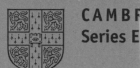

CAMBRIDGE FIRST CERTIFICATE
Grammar and Usage

NEW EDITION

Bob Obee

RIDGE
UNIVERSITY PRESS

PUBLISHED BY THE PRESS SYNDICATE OF THE UNIVERSITY OF CAMBRIDGE
The Pitt Building, Trumpington Street, Cambridge CB2 1RP, United Kingdom

CAMBRIDGE UNIVERSITY PRESS
The Edinburgh Building, Cambridge CB2 2RU, United Kingdom
40 West 20th Street, New York, NY 10011–4211, USA
10 Stamford Road, Oakleigh, Melbourne 3166, Australia

First published 1995
Second edition 1998

Printed in the United Kingdom at the University Press, Cambridge

ISBN 0 521 62486 X Student's Book
ISBN 0 521 62485 1 Teacher's Book

Contents

Map of the book

Acknowledgements

I would like to thank Sue O'Connell for her invaluable guidance and also Charlotte Adams and Niki Browne at Cambridge University Press for their support and hard work in helping to revise this book.

From the first edition: I would like to thank the Series Editor, Sue O'Connell, for her invaluable comments and guidance, my editor Jeanne McCarten for her support and timely deadline reminders, Geraldine Mark, Brigit Viney and all the staff at Cambridge University Press involved in the production of the book. I should also like to thank especially Paul Carne, Jean Greenwood, Chris Hare, Ian Johnson, Laura Matthews, Keith Mitchell, Clare West and Simon Williams for their insightful comments and all teachers and students involved in piloting the material.

The author and publishers are grateful to the following individuals and institutions for permission to use copyright material in *Cambridge First Certificate Grammar and Usage*. While every effort has been made, it has not been possible to identify the sources of all material used and in such cases the publishers would welcome information from copyright holders.

Cartoons

Cartoons 1, 3, 5, and 6 on p. 47 reprinted by kind permission of the *Spectator*; cartoon 4 on p. 47 by Hector Breeze © Hector Breeze; Garfield cartoon on p. 58 reproduced by permission of PAWS, INC.

Photographs

Photograph on p. 41 from the *Bank of England Museum: A Souvenir Guide* © Governor and Company of the Bank of England; photographs on p. 73 of Sarah Ferguson, Mikhail Gorbachev (photograph © Vitaly Armand/AFP), Diana, Princess of Wales, Mao Tse-Tung, kangaroo, George Bush, Sydney Opera House (photograph by Cleland Rimmer): Popperfoto Ltd; photographs on p. 73 of Anthony Hopkins (in *The Remains of the Day*): The Ronald Grant Archive/ © 1993 Columbia Pictures Industries; Jack Nicholson (in *One Flew Over the Cuckoo's Nest*): The Ronald Grant Archive; photograph on p. 73 of sun dial: Sam Greenhill/ Sally and Richard Greenhill; photograph on p. 73 of joy-stick, floppy disk and mouse: Sally and Richard Greenhill; photograph on p. 73 of egg-timer: Pictor International Ltd; logos on p. 73 by courtesy of Esso UK plc, Jaguar Cars Limited, BP Oil International; photograph on p. 89 of Brian Blessed: Gary Trotter/Rex Features Ltd; photographs on p. 109, 2: Interstock/Spectrum; 3: R. Symons/Spectrum; 5: Dan Smith/Allsport UK Ltd; 6, 7, 8: Sporting Pictures.

We are unable to trace the following copyright holders and would be grateful for any information that would enable us to do so: Photograph on p. 59 of Rosamond Richardson; photographs of diving tank, snorkel and flippers on p. 73: Mark Gascoigne; logo on p. 73: La Chemise Lacoste; photograph on p. 109 of skier: F. Witmer/Stockfile, 1: (photograph by J. Carter); 4: Keith Mayhew.

Photograph permissions researched by Diane May

Text extracts

Adapted advertisement on p. 7 reprinted with permission from Brooke Bond Foods Ltd; extract on p.14 adapted from *The Dictionary of Idioms* © 1992 Linda and Roger Flavell, published by Kyle Cathie Ltd; extract on p. 23 adapted from *The Hip and Thigh Diet* by Rosemary Conley, published by Arrow Books Ltd; all entries on p. 25 and entry for *make* on p. 133 from *Collins COBUILD English Dictionary* © William Collins & Sons 1987, with the permission of HarperCollins Publishers Ltd; extract on p. 31 adapted from a Springboard Internet Services Limited advertisement for LineOne in *The Sunday Times Magazine*; extract on p. 32 and extracts 3 and 4 on p. 68 adapted from *The Guinness Book of Records 1987* © Guinness Publishing Ltd 1986; extracts 1, 2, 5 and 6 on p. 68 adapted from *The Guinness Book of Records 1994* © Guinness Publishing Ltd 1993; extract on p. 33 adapted from *The Long Day Wanes* by Anthony Burgess, published by William Heinemann Ltd, 1994; extracts on pp. 33 and 39–40 adapted from 'The Mekong River' by Thomas O'Neill from *National Geographic*, February 1993; extract on p. 41 adapted from the *Bank of England Museum: A Souvenir Guide* © Governor and Company of the Bank of England; extract on p. 48 adapted from Monarch Airlines *Inflight* magazine; extract on p. 56 adapted from *Essential Thailand* by Christine Osborne, reproduced with the permission of AA Publishing; extract on p. 57 adapted from *Learn English in Britain*, published by ARELS – the Association of Recognised English Language Services; article on p. 58 from the *Daily Mail* © Daily Mail/Solo; extract on p. 59 from *Vegetarian Meals – A Sainsbury Cookbook* by Rosamund Richardson, published by Martin Books; extract on p. 74 adapted from the Introduction to *The Day of the Triffids* by John Wyndham (Penguin Books, 1987) © Penguin Books Ltd, 1987; extracts on pp. 80 and 142 adapted from *The Guinness Book of Oddities* © Guinness Publishing Ltd and Geoff Tibballs 1995 (GUINNESS is a registered trade mark); adapted advertisement on p. 82 © The Leisure Study Group Pty Limited; extract on p. 88 adapted from 'Wide Open Wyoming' by Thomas J. Abercrombie from *National Geographic*, January 1993; article on p. 89 adapted from the *Evening Standard* 23/2/93 © Evening Standard/Solo; extract on p. 96 adapted from 'What a Web we Weave' by Victor Keegan from the *Guardian* 13/5/97; extract on pp. 103–4 adapted from *Athenscope – The Weekly Guide to What's On in Athens*, Issue No 25; extract on pp. 104–5 adapted from 'Nightmare on a Dark Ocean' by John Dyson from *Reader's Digest* April 1997; translation errors on p. 110 © Addison-Wesley Publishing Co Inc; extract on pp. 110–11 adapted from 'The Dawn of Humans' by Rick Gore from *National Geographic* May 1997; extract 5 on p. 112 and extract (e) on p. 119 from the *Guardian*; extract 2 on p. 112 and extract (a) on p. 119 from the *Independent*; extract on p. 118 adapted from 'Say Baa Baa to Bad Driving' by Jane Szita from *The Sunday Times* 28/7/96; extract (c) on p. 119 from the *Star* (Malaysia); extract on pp. 124–5 adapted from *Strange but True* by Tim Healey, published by Octopus Books (a division of Reed Consumer Books Ltd); extract on p. 125 adapted from 'The Greek Islands' from *Bitter Lemons* by Lawrence Durrell, published by Faber & Faber; entries for *tell* and *try* on p. 133 adapted from the *Longman Dictionary of Contemporary English* (new edition) published by Longman Group UK Ltd 1987; extract on p. 143 adapted from 'Minders' by Daniel Jeffreys from *Marie Claire* July 1997; extract on p.146 adapted from *World's Greatest Unsolved Crimes* by Roger Boa and N. Blundell, published by Octopus Books.

Text permissions researched by Nikki Burton.

Illustrations

Helen Humphries: pp. 3, 29, 30, 50 (bottom), 82; Bill Piggins: pp. 11, 79, 123; Vicky Lowe: pp. 12, (top), 100; Amanda MacPhail: pp. 12 (bottom), 13, 23, 31, 47 (bottom), 49, 56, 65, 66, 74, 81, 87, 88, 96, 104, 117, 118, 124, 140; Paul Collicut: pp. 21, 63, 116; Shaun Williams: p. 22; Angela Joliffe: p. 38; Jeremy Long: pp. 47 (top right), 126; Tony Healey: p. 50 (top); Tracy Rich: pp. 55, 98; Jerry Collins: p. 75; Tess Stone: p. 86; Sue Hillwood-Harris: p. 102; Paul Dickinson: p. 106; Mike Ogden: p. 131; Edward McLachlan: p. 139.

Facsimile artwork by Kevin McGeoghegan
Cover illustration by Annabel Wright

Introduction

Who is this book for?

This book provides grammar and usage practice for students preparing for Paper 3 of the Cambridge FCE exam. It can also, however, be used as a general grammar and usage workbook for students at this level. It aims to combine both general communicative grammar work with exam training; to serve students as a valuable grammar reference resource and, through its task-based approach, to improve students' grammar learning strategies.

How is the book organised?

The book is organised into eighteen units. Each unit focuses on a particular grammar area that is likely to be tested in Paper 3 of the FCE exam.

How is each unit organised?

Each unit is divided into four sections. The unit starts with a **Lead-in** section which introduces the language area to be looked at and sets students problem-solving tasks through which they can begin to explore some of the grammar and usage issues.

This is then followed by an interactive **Reference** section which, as well as highlighting the key grammar points and usage contrasts, requires students to fill in tables and grids, complete sets of examples and do a variety of exercises so that they become involved in the compiling of their own reference resource.

The third section is for **Communicative practice**. Students are encouraged to use the language which has been introduced in the two previous sections through a wide variety of lively and engaging task frameworks. The tasks involve contexts which encourage students to engage more personally with the language by talking about experiences and sharing opinions, deductions and what they know of the world with other students.

The unit ends with the **Exam focus** section. In each unit one or two types of exam question from Paper 3 are looked at. The ways in which the language can be tested by each question type are presented and students are given useful exam tips on how to tackle each question. The Exam focus questions can be done in class or at home and all the Exam focus sections taken together provide thorough exam training for the Use of English section of the Cambridge First Certificate examination.

How should the material be used?

The course can either be used in strict unit sequence or in a different order to coincide with a teacher's main course priorities and aims.

Each unit provides approximately two hours' class work. There is scope for flexibility in timings as certain tasks in the Reference sections and tasks in the Exam focus sections can be set for homework. The Teacher's Book also gives several useful ideas for follow-up tasks to main tasks.

What special features are there?

- The book begins with a **Foundation unit** which encourages students to think about their own grammar learning priorities as they approach the exam and raises some key issues about learning grammar and keeping grammar notes.

- Each unit begins with a **Summary** which highlights the grammar points and exam questions to be covered.

- The book includes numerous **Exam Tips** which indicate to students how best to tackle the different types of exam question.

- The book contains over forty stimulating **Communicative practice** activities to animate the grammar learning experience in the classroom.

- The book uses a great deal of authentic material so that students can learn grammar through genuine contexts.

- The **Teacher's Book** provides notes on typical student problems with each language area covered, practical suggestions on how best to exploit the material and guidelines on timing.

- The book finishes with a **Review unit** which provides a thorough revision session on each of the main question types in Paper 3.

Foundation unit

Language focus: what does learning grammar involve?; making grammar notes; ways of learning grammar; using this book; types of exam questions

LEAD-IN

Each unit in this book begins with a Lead-in section which will encourage you to explore what you already know about the grammar to be covered in the unit.

Read the questions below and choose the answers that match most closely your feelings about learning grammar. Then plot your answers on the graph by drawing a circle around the letters of your answers and joining them together with a line.

1 Grammar is

   A necessary but boring.
   B challenging and fun.

2 Making grammar mistakes

   A is the worst thing a learner can do.
   B can often help you to learn something.

3 Learning to use grammar correctly means

   A doing grammar exercises.
   B speaking and writing.

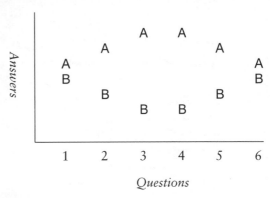

4 The notes you make on grammar

   A can never be as good as a reference book.
   B may make rules and examples more memorable.

5 The best way to learn grammar is

   A to learn rules by heart.
   B to see grammar working in real language situations.

6 Grammar is

   A cold and mathematical.
   B warm and human.

Now draw the shape of this line between points 'x' and 'y' in the face.

What does this tell you about your feelings about grammar? If your answers were all A, or a mixture of A and B, imagine what your picture would look like if they were all B.

Compare your picture with that of another student. Discuss the similarities and differences between them.

REFERENCE

The Reference sections in this book will give you concise explanations and lots of examples of specific grammar points. You will almost certainly, however, want to keep your own grammar notebook as you work towards the exam.

Below are extracts taken from two students' grammar notebooks. For each of the grammar points, decide which student you think has made the better notes and think about why. Discuss your answers with another student.

Student A   *Student B*

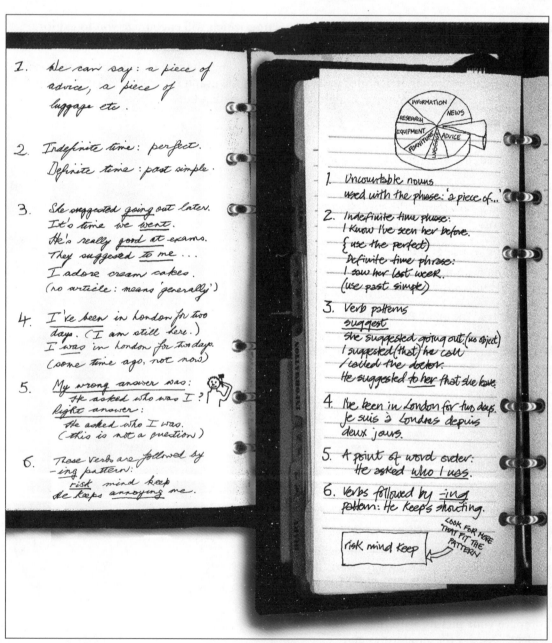

COMMUNICATIVE PRACTICE

The Communicative practice sections in this book will involve you in completing two or three tasks with other students. In doing these tasks you will have an opportunity to practise the language looked at in earlier sections in communicative situations.

1 Grammar activities and goals

As a student who is keen to learn grammar and as one who is approaching the First Certificate exam, choose from the list below the five most important things for you.

1　Revising grammar rules and looking at examples.
2　Seeing how grammar works in real texts and contexts.
3　Tips on how to learn grammar from reference books.
4　Learning how specific grammar points are tested in the First Certificate exam.
5　Communicating in speaking and writing, using the grammar you have learnt.
6　Getting specific tips on how to tackle grammar questions in Paper 3.
7　Doing grammar practice exercises.
8　Practising exam-type questions.
9　Checking how much grammar you already know.
10　Talking about yourself, other people and the world around us in English.

Now think about your choices. Do they tell you anything about your strengths and weaknesses as a learner of English? Discuss your choices with another student to see if you agree.

2 Using this book

As you work through the units in this book, you'll be doing all the things mentioned in Task 1. Look back at the ten types of activity in Task 1. With another student, try and work out which types of activity you'll be doing in each section (Lead-in, Reference, Communicative practice and Exam focus). You might like to look at Unit 3 as a sample unit. You may want to put the same activity into more than one section.

Lead-in:　　　　　　　　　*1*.............................

Reference:　　　　　　　　.............................

Communicative practice:　.............................

Exam focus:　　　　　　　.............................

You should now have an idea of how the book works and how best to make it work for you.

EXAM FOCUS

This section of each unit focuses on how the language area presented in the unit is likely to be tested in the exam. In each section, one or two exam-type questions will be looked at and useful tips given on how to approach the question.

Question types

The five following types of question occur in Paper 3 of the First Certificate exam. Look at each type of question and discuss with another student exactly what you have to do in each one. Working with your partner, write instructions for each type of question and then complete the tasks.

Part 1: Multiple-choice cloze (based on a text)

Herbert Frein was (1) ..*educated*.. at the University of Nottingham. He moved to the United

States in 1950 and (2) .... up a post at Westgate College in Baltimore.

1	A learnt	B educated	C lectured	D passed
2	A got	B went	C took	D looked

Part 2: Open cloze (based on a text)

The number of people who wanted to join the navy was very high, but the number applying to

join the air force was (1) ......*even*...... higher. It is difficult to say exactly why this was the case

but one reason (2) .... have been that conscripts were thinking of career opportunities

after service.

Part 3: Key-word transformation

1 I haven't heard from my sister in ages.

It has *been ages since I* heard from my sister.   **since**

2 The meeting took place in France last week.

The meeting .... France last week.   **held**

Part 4: Error correction (based on a text)

1 My first day at my new college in England was a little tiring   ✔

2 and frustrating both. I arrived early because we had to go   *both*

3 and get our timetables and sort out things such like registration

4 for extra English classes and joining the library.

Part 5: Word formation (based on a text)

We have always been particularly (1) .....*proud*..... of the commitment we show   PRIDE

our customers and the (2) .... they give us in return.   LOYAL

Unit 1 **The present**

Language focus: uses of the present simple and present continuous to talk about present time

Exam focus: error correction and multiple-choice cloze questions

LEAD-IN

1 The text below is about the increasing number of people that are becoming vegetarians. Before you read it answer these questions.

- Are there any vegetarians in your country?
- Are more people in your country becoming vegetarians?

Discuss these questions with another student.

What are the two main kinds of reasons for people being or becoming vegetarians in your country? Choose from this list. Then compare your answers with another student.

economic   moral   religious   political
health   weight   none of these

2 Read the text and the questions about the numbered examples. Choose the right answers.

Healthy eating for vegetarians

Today more and more people (1) **are becoming** concerned about their diet, general fitness and lifestyle. Many (2) **are turning** away from meat and are starting to look for healthy alternatives. For some, becoming a vegetarian has provided an answer. Vegetables, fruit and pulses are healthy foods which can be made into hundreds of tasty meals; they also (3) **give** you plenty of energy and vitality to keep you going throughout the day.

If you (4) **are thinking** of taking the plunge, then you might be interested in a useful leaflet produced by Batchelors, *Healthy Eating for Vegetarians*, which gives practical hints and tips on becoming a vegetarian. Fortunately, this (5) **doesn't mean** hours of slaving in the kitchen nor lots of menu planning. The two delicious snacks below (6) **take** less than ten minutes to prepare. Batchelors (7) **produce** lots of convenient and tasty foods, for those who (8) **don't eat** meat – just look out for the V symbol on packs, which means they've been approved by the Vegetarian Society. Batchelors (9) **are** also **offering** for this month only, 10 per cent off all vegetarian products.

(adapted from a Batchelors advertisement)

1 In Examples 1 and 2 the present continuous tense is used because the writer is talking about

   A a permanent situation.
   B a changing / developing situation.

2 In Examples 3, 5 and 6 the present simple tense is used because the writer is talking about

   A general truths.
   B something that happens every day.

3 In Example 4 the present continuous tense is used because the writer is talking about

   A a repeated or habitual action.
   B something happening around the time of writing.

4 In Example 7 the present simple tense is used because the writer is talking about

   A a permanent situation.
   B a developing situation.
   C a temporary situation.

5 In Example 8 the present simple tense is used because the writer is talking about

   A a temporary situation.
   B a repeated or habitual action.

6 In Example 9 the present continuous tense is used because the writer is talking about

   A a permanent situation.
   B a temporary situation.
   C a developing situation.

REFERENCE

Form

Present simple

Affirmative	*Negative*
I live, she lives, etc.	I do not (don't) live, she does not (doesn't) live, etc.

Question	*Short answers*
Do you live?	Yes, I do. No, I don't.

Present continuous

Affirmative	*Negative*
I am (I'm) living, etc.	I am not (I'm not) living, etc.

Question	*Short answers*
Are you living?	Yes, I am. No, I'm not.

Uses

Present simple	Present continuous
To talk about repeated or habitual actions. Our meetings **don't usually start** until about 4.15.	To talk about actions which are in progress at or around the time of speaking. Look! The meeting **is starting**. We'd better go in.
To talk about situations which are permanent or last for a long period of time. 'Where **do** you **work**?' 'I **work** for Santax, a firm that **makes** mechanical toys.'	To talk about situations which are temporary, but not necessarily happening at the time of speaking. 'What **are** you **working** on at the moment?' 'A report for my boss.'
To talk about general truths / facts / scientific laws. Plants **do not grow** well if they are kept in the dark.	To talk about situations which are in the process of developing or changing. Michael **is growing** so quickly you won't recognise him the next time you see him.

Verbs not typically used in the present continuous

The verbs below are not usually used in the continuous tense:

- like, want, wish
- agree, believe, care, know, mean, remember, suppose, understand
- look like, resemble, seem
- belong, contain, need, owe, own
- hear, see, smell, taste.

With the verbs **hear, see, smell** and **taste, can** is used to give the idea of *an action in progress*.

Can you **taste** the garlic in the soup? (Not: Are you tasting . . . ?)
The windscreen is so dirty I **can hardly see** the road.

1 Give a short definition of the words below, using a verb from the list above.

Example: 'Regret' is the feeling you have when you wish things had happened differently.

1 'Property' is something ....

2 'Contents' are the things that ....

3 'Hard of hearing' describes someone ....

4 'A debt' is something ....

5 'Flavour' is what something ....

6 'Similarity' is a word used when someone / something ....

....

7 'A difference of opinion' is when two ....

8 'A synonym' is a word ....

Time words and phrases

1 The time word or phrase in a sentence is very often a clue to which tense to use. The words and phrases in the box below are nearly always used with the *present simple* tense to talk about present time.

always	as a rule	each / every time	ever	generally	how often . . . ?
most days	never	normally	once a (week)	rarely	regularly
sometimes	usually				

*The bus **usually** arrives at ten past the hour.*
*Our hotel does not, **as a rule**, cater for weddings.*

2 When talking about present time, the following words and phrases usually indicate that the *present continuous* tense, rather than the present simple, should be used.

at present	at the moment	currently	for now	for the time being
temporarily	this (morning)	today		

*Our phone isn't working **at the moment**.*

2 Underline the time expression in each of the sentences below and then complete them by putting the verb in brackets into the correct tense.

1 Each time I .... her to go out, she comes up with some clever excuse. (ask)

2 My sister .... some money as a lifeguard at the moment until she starts university.   (earn)

3 We didn't think Tony would be home. .... he .... today? (work / not)

4 .... he always .... his temper like that when he's losing a game?   (lose)

5 The bank .... normally .... open this late, but we're working different hours up to Christmas.   (stay / not)

6 We .... for now – we've decided we can't afford it. (move / not)

7 She .... better than ever this season.   (run)

8 .... you ever .... anything out of the ordinary? (do / not)

COMMUNICATIVE PRACTICE

1 They look the type

Look at the two columns of words between the pictures. Match a word on the left to one on the right to make a new noun and then match this phrase to one of the definitions below.

party	climbers
sun	fanatics
fitness	birds
telly	goers
back	packers
home	addicts
social	worshippers

1 .... are people who go out to parties and socialise a lot.

2 .... are people who want to improve their social position.

3 .... are people who spend a lot of time tanning themselves.

4 .... are people who spend a lot of their free time exercising.

5 .... are people who love to travel and see new places.

6 .... are people who do nothing but sit and watch television.

7 .... are people who spend most of their time at home.

Look at the pictures and, with another student, try and work out who is married to whom. Look for two people who clearly have something in common.

Example:

A: *I think the man who is wearing the fur coat and who looks as if he's having a really good time is probably married to the woman who's holding a drink.*

B: *What do they have in common?*

A: *They like going to parties.*

B: *Yeah, they're probably the 'party goers'.*

2 Customs around the world

Look at the map of the world and the pictures. Working with another student, find your way around the world as quickly as you can. Explain the custom connected with the picture in each country that you pass through.

Example: *In Canada Eskimos rub noses as a greeting and a sign of affection.*

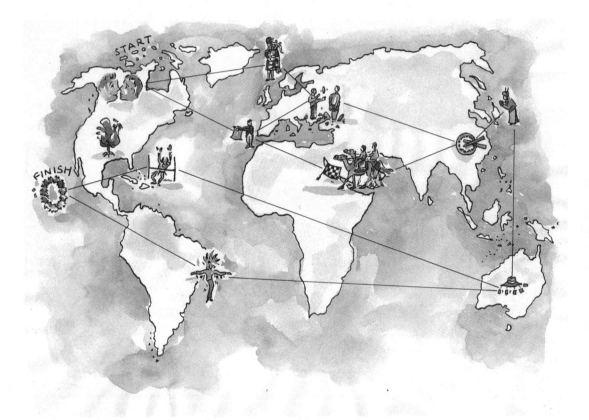

EXAM FOCUS

EXAM TIP 1

Lines and sentences

Read the whole passage in the error correction task in Part 4 through first to get an idea what it is about. In this task you have to decide whether each *line* is correct or contains an unnecessary word. You must, however, read each line as part of the *sentence* it is in to decide whether an unnecessary word has been used or not.

12

1 Error correction

Read the text below and look carefully at each line. Some of the lines are correct, and some have a word which should not be there. If a line is correct, put a tick by it. If a line has a word which should not be there, write the word at the end of the line. There are two examples at the beginning (0 and 00).

My home town

0   My home 'town' is a small village in the southern Alps of France called   ✓

00 Montpasse. In the past most people were farmers but today people are earn   *are*

1   their living from tourism and small businesses. Montpasse is being a pretty

2   town with an old castle and wonderful views of the mountains. The sun

3   shines the most days, even in winter when the weather is perfect for skiing.

4   It is a great place to grow up as a child. There are wonderful fields of corn

5   where can children play and beautifully clear streams and rivers just outside

6   the town where do you see fish jumping out of the water. On a hot summer's

7   day the cool water of those streams and rivers is looking like an oasis. My

8   favourite childhood memories are of such afternoons with my friends. The

9   winter sports are fantastic too and a pair of skis is all you have need for

10 hours of fun. I haven't been back to my village for a while but all I have to

11 do is think of home and I do almost taste the fresh air and feel the gentle wind.

12 I am living in England often now because of my work. I would love to go

13 home this summer and spend long lazy days by the rivers. I have not the

14 money; it's a question of finding the time to get away. I am suppose we all

15 miss the place we grew up in and we all want to go back some time.

EXAM TIP 2

Don't distract me!

In the multiple-choice cloze task in Part 1 only one out of four possible answers is correct; the other three wrong answers are called 'distractors'. When you complete this task you need to think about i) what parts of speech *could* fit in the gap and then ii) which alternative fits in the context of the text. If you consider each possible answer from both these points of view, you are less likely to be distracted and more likely to pick the correct answer.

2 Multiple-choice cloze

Read the text below and decide which answer A, B, C or D best fits each space. There is
an example at the beginning (0).

Advertisements

Perhaps the most creative (0) ....*use*....... of language in newspapers is in the
advertisements. The writers have to catch and (1) .... the reader's attention. They
often (2) .... this with a play on words. You read the words and understand them
one way and then suddenly you (3) .... that another interpretation is possible.
Through that ambiguity the advertisement has caught your attention – and the advertiser
(4) .... you'll buy the product.

Under the picture of a new car are the words: 'Not another family saloon'. The dual
interpretation of that phrase is dependent on how it is pronounced. Misread it by putting the
stress on the second word thereby projecting a message the advertiser would clearly not
want, and this (5) .... you look again and pay conscious attention to the alternative
message.

Advertising copywriters frequently (6) .... use of idioms. One advertisement
showed girls wearing different coloured jeans, but none the traditional blue ones. Underneath
were the words: 'Jeanius is (7) .... ideas out of the blue'. On one level, that
(8) .... the jeans are not ordinary blue jeans but ones in a range of colours. But there
is also the suggestion that these new jeans are a sudden piece of inspiration, a stroke of
genius. 'Out of the blue' is an idiom which means 'quite unexpectedly' and genius often
(9) .... getting a brilliant idea suddenly. That's very clever, but it's not quite the end
of it, because it's not genius they are (10) .... about, but jeanius. That is another play
on words; the product they are selling, after all, is a pair of jeans.

(adapted from Linda and Roger Flavell, *The Dictionary of Idioms*)

0	A point	B exercise	C use	D practice
1	A maintain	B hold	C remain	D pay
2	A have	B make	C succeed	D do
3	A aware	B realise	C indicate	D wonder
4	A hopes	B wishes	C sees	D makes
5	A tells	B makes	C causes	D forces
6	A have	B do	C make	D get
7	A having	B thinking	C making	D arriving
8	A means	B tells	C seems	D pretends
9	A compares	B is	C contains	D involves
10	A talking	B saying	C telling	D meaning

Unit 2 Modals 1

Language focus: uses of modal verbs of ability and permission (in the present and past)
and modal verbs of obligation and possibility (in the present)

Exam focus: open cloze and key-word transformation questions

LEAD-IN

1 Read the jokes and, with another student, find the punch line – in a–i below – that completes each joke.

1 During a lesson on the benefits of eating healthy food an enthusiastic teacher asked, 'Can anyone name five things that contain milk?'

2 A motorist and his wife had had a quarrel and hadn't spoken for hours. Suddenly the man saw a donkey in a field. 'Must be a relative of yours,' he said.

3 At a buffet dinner a husband said to his wife, 'You can't be going back for dessert again. That makes five times. Aren't you ashamed?'

4 At the sight of a submarine a baby sardine quickly hid behind its mother. 'You needn't be afraid,' she said.

5 On arriving home holding a brightly-coloured bag, a husband asked, 'What do you think I might have here for the one I love best?'

6 A struggling newspaper reporter asked his editor, 'Do you think I ought to put more fire into my stories?'

7 A maths teacher was explaining to students what they had to do to get the answer to this problem: 'You have ten fingers. Suppose you had three less. What would you have?'

8 A bookshop assistant, eager for a quick sale, approached a student and said, 'I guarantee that this book can do half your work for you.'

9 After hearing much yelling and screaming, a father burst into his sons' room to find them fighting on the floor. 'Okay, who started this?' he asked.

a) 'It's only a can of people.'

b) 'No, vice versa.'

c) 'You did. You told him he could hit me back,' replied the elder son.

d) 'Butter, cream, cheese and two cows.'

e) 'No music lessons.'

f) 'Not really. I just say that I'm getting it for you.'

g) 'Cigars, razor blades and a new electric drill.'

h) 'Yes, by marriage.'

i) 'Great, I'll take two of them.'

2 Each of the jokes in Task 1 contains a *modal verb*. Modal verbs are used in front of the main verb in a sentence. They can express ideas such as the possibility, necessity or certainty of an action happening. Look back at the jokes and underline the modal verb in each one. Then check your answers with another student.

Example: <u>*Can*</u> *anyone name five things that contain milk?*

3 Now discuss with another student which of the meanings below is expressed by the modal verb in each joke. Write the number of the joke next to one of the meanings.

1 ability (of a person/thing to do something) ....

2 necessity (Is it necessary or unnecessary?) ....

3 permission (Is the person allowed to do something?) ....

4 possibility (How sure is the speaker?) ....

REFERENCE

Form

Affirmative	*Negative*
I can, etc.	I cannot (can't), etc.

Question	*Short answers*
Can you?	Yes, I can. No, I can't.

1 Modal verbs do not change form. They do not take an auxiliary in the question and negative form.

2 Modal verbs are followed by the infinitive without **to**.

   *You **must arrive** on time.*
   *You **needn't bother**.*

3 We cannot use two modal verbs together: for example not *She should can go*. The second idea is expressed by a phrase such as **be able to** or **be allowed to**.

   *She should **be able to** go.*

Uses

Modal verbs express a number of different kinds of meaning. One verb can often express more than one kind of meaning. For example:

He can play really well. (ability)
Can I come in now? (permission)
You can't be serious. (possibility)

1 First see how many of the sentences you can complete by choosing the correct answer from the verbs in brackets. Then study Sections A and B and decide on your final answer.

1 Stephanie .... hear someone approaching and quickly hid behind the door.   (was able to / could)

2 'Could I borrow the car, Dad?' 'No, you ....'
   (can't / couldn't)

3 The lifeguard arrived and .... save us.
   (could / managed to)

4 .... your lawyer go with you yesterday?   (Couldn't / Could)

5 No one .... see the prisoner since Friday.
   (could / has been allowed to)

6 The people that had been queuing outside the shop .... go in early.   (could / were allowed to)

7 I .... make any phone calls for over an hour.
   (can't have / haven't been able to)

8 As we approached we .... smell something good cooking.
   (could / were able to)

A *Ability:* can, could, be able to

1 Can and **cannot / can't** are more commonly used to talk about ability to do something in the present than **be (not) able to**.

*Mum **can't drive** at the moment because her leg is in plaster.*
*The doctor **can see** you right away, if you have the time.*

2 To talk about someone's ability to do something in the past we use **could, be able to** and **manage to** as follows:

General ability (to do something at any time)	could couldn't could you? *I **could** talk before I **could** walk.* ***Could** you really run that fast at school?*
Specific ability (to do something on one occasion)	couldn't was / were (not) able to (not) managed to *I **was able to** see the doctor without an appointment.* *Did you **manage to** phone the boss this morning?* (not: *could*) *I **couldn't** join the sailing club then – I was too young.*

NOTE: The verbs **see, hear, feel, smell, taste** and **understand** are an exception and are used with **could** to talk about specific ability.

*The guard **could smell** smoke but didn't know where it was from.*

3 To talk about ability with perfect and future forms, the **be able to** structure is used.

*The police **have not been able to** identify the body yet.*
*When **will** he **be able to** come home, doctor?*

B *Permission:* can, could, may, be allowed to

1 When asking for permission in the present we usually use **can** and **could**. **Could** is less direct than **can**. **May** can be used but is quite formal.

When giving permission we nearly always use **can**. Again **may** can be used but sounds rather formal.

*'**Could** I leave early as I've got an interview?' 'Of course you **can**.'*
*'**Can** I call you back? I'm in a meeting at the moment.*
*'**May** I use your phone, please?*

When talking about whether something is permitted or not we use **can / can't** and **be (not) allowed to**.

*Guests **can** leave their keys at reception or take them with them.*
*Don't you know you're **not allowed to** smoke during take-off?*

2 To talk about permission in the past:

General permission	could / couldn't was / were (not) allowed to
	*As a child I **could** always stay up late at weekends.*
	*We **weren't allowed to** wear what we liked to school when we were young.*
Permission in specific situations	was / were (not) allowed to couldn't
	*The candidate **was allowed to** ask a few questions.* (not: *could*)
	*The security police told us we **couldn't** wait inside the airport because someone important was arriving.*

3 When talking about permission with future and perfect forms **be allowed to** must be used.

*You **will not be allowed to** bring notes into the exam.*
*He's **never been allowed to** travel alone.*

C *Obligation and necessity:* must, have to, should, ought to, needn't

2 Imagine someone is talking about going to a meeting. Match a sentence from the column on the left to one on the right which explains it.

1 You ought to go.   a) It would be a waste of time for you to go.
2 You must go.   b) That's the company rule.
3 You have to be there.   c) No one is forcing you to go.
4 You don't have to go.   d) That's an order.
5 You needn't go.   e) It would really help you.
6 You mustn't go.   f) It wouldn't be right.

Now check your answers by reading the information below.

1 Must is normally used when the sense of obligation comes from the speaker / writer.
*You **must** stop smoking for the sake of your health.*

Have to is used when the obligation comes from someone else or an external authority.
*We **have to** be out of the room by 12.00 – that's the hotel rule.*

Have to, however, has to be used when talking about obligation with future, past and perfect meanings.
*There were no seats left so some of the audience **had to stand**.*
*We **will have to** be going now in case it rains.*
*He's **had to** give up his job for health reasons.*

2 **Mustn't** is used to express strong disapproval, or that something is forbidden.
*You **mustn't** keep annoying your father. He is trying to work.*

Don't have to is used to express the idea that there is no law, rule or requirement to make you do something.
*I adore Saturday mornings when I **don't have to** get up for work.*

Needn't expresses the speaker's opinion that something isn't necessary.
*You **needn't** worry about the boat trip – it only lasts ten minutes.*

3 **Should** and **ought to** express milder obligation; they are often used when giving advice or talking about people's responsibilities.
*I really **ought to** be getting home – my daughter is expecting me.*
*You **should** always keep receipts when you buy large items.*

D Possibility, probability and certainty

3 Complete each of the rules below and their accompanying examples with a word from the box.

must	can	may	can't	might not	could	couldn't

1 (a) .... is used when the speaker is certain that something is true.

(b) .... is used when the speaker believes something is impossible or is certain that something isn't true.

That (c) .... be the Paris train – it's not due for hours.

I (d) .... be missing a page – this doesn't make sense.

2 **Should** and **ought to** can express the idea that something is probable or likely.

*You **should** be receiving a cheque from us in a few days.*

3 (a) .... is used to talk about the general possibility of something.

Leave early as the roads (b) .... be especially busy at that time.

May, **might** and **could** are used to express the idea of possibility in specific situations.

(c) .... can indicate stronger possibility than **might** or (d) .... and is not used to ask questions.

May not and **might not** are used to express the idea that it is possible that something is not true. **Could not** means that in your opinion something is not hypothetically possible.

*You **may** well be right about the cost but I'm still going.*

I (e) .... not be going to see her now that something's come up.

(f) .... he be using your credit card without your knowing?

4 **Complete the following sentences with an appropriate modal verb form.**

1 You .... possibly go out looking like that.

2 Your friend .... be able to get seats without too much trouble.

3 You .... bother phoning, just turn up about sixish.

4 .... you really buy a house that cheaply in those days?

5 I'm afraid I .... get petty cash requests approved by the manager.

6 He .... be joking! The car's not worth anywhere near that much.

7 It's not a good time to visit Britain. The weather .... be awful at this time of year.

8 Only the press .... visit the crash site yesterday.

9 Your parents .... stop you going to the concert, although I can understand why they're worried.

10 Martin .... need the car. Why don't you ask to borrow it?

COMMUNICATIVE PRACTICE

1 Treasure hunt

Look at the map opposite and find the place labelled 'Start here'. Then follow the instructions on the document below which was written by Pirate Scragg. They will tell you how to find his buried treasure.

~ *The treasure of Pirate Scragg* ~

Go to the point where the bird wouldn't stop if it flew straight to the pond.

And from here go to the place where you ought to cross the road.

Now take the quickest route round a place where you can sink but can't swim.

To a place where you can find smoke without fire.

From here go to a place where a pirate's feet might not touch the ground.

And then to a place where you can always expect to see white water.

Now pass an old pirate who needn't be feared.

To a place where you may hear singing and ringing.

Now you must retrace your steps with the line of a thick black pen.

Look at the shape you have drawn, and this shape should reveal the location of the treasure in one of the places you didn't have to visit.

2 What's the law?

Look at the pictures below which illustrate eight different situations in Britain. Then look at the phrases in the box and, with another student, decide which phrase tells you something about the law in each situation. Then work out what the law might be.

Useful language when talking about the law:		
have to/don't have to	(not) be allowed to	can/cannot

legal limit	age of 16 or 18	age of 17	no law
licence	70	six months	age of 16

Example: *Picture 1 – licence.*

You have to buy a television licence each year if you own or rent a television.

Now you know the law in Britain, discuss with your partner whether it is different or the same in your country.

EXAM FOCUS

1 Open cloze

The text below is adapted from a book called *The Hip and Thigh Diet*. Here the author is explaining how to use the diet and talking about the results you can expect.

Read the text and think of the word which best fits each space. Use only *one* word in each space. Then check your answers with another student. There is an example at the beginning (0).

The Hip and Thigh Diet

We think you (0) ....should.... initially follow the menu selections provided here as a basic guide but as you become more familiar with the fat content of all foods you will soon be (1) .... to make up your own selections.

You have (2) .... given a list of strictly forbidden foods so that you (3) .... make a definite resolution before you begin the diet: 'I (4) .... ban them totally from my life!' If you are going to cheat and put bars of chocolate or packets of salted peanuts into your cupboard to eat when no one's around then you really (5) .... to give this book to someone else. This diet, (6) .... followed properly, will help you to achieve the kind of figure you never dreamed possible but there is only one person who (7) .... actually make it work for you – and that's YOU. You're the one that (8) .... to stick to it.

You will probably be very pleasantly surprised at the amount of food you are allowed by the diet. You'll find yourself on a strict diet without (9) .... to suffer in the process. My volunteers really loved it and they (10) .... not believe they could actually lose weight yet eat so much.

(adapted from Rosemary Conley, *The Hip and Thigh Diet*)

2 Key-word transformation

a Read sentences 1 to 10 and think about which modal verb in the box below expresses the same idea as the bold phrase in each sentence. There may be more than one possible answer.

should	needn't	might not	(be) able to	(be) allowed to	mustn't	can't
have to	must	✓could	don't have to	ought to	(be) not allowed to	

Example: **There's a chance** the hurricane will hit northern towns tomorrow. *could*

1 **There's no need** for you to bring a present as well.

   You .... bring a present as well.

2 I'm surprised **permission was given** for Mrs Jones to have the day off.

   I'm surprised Mrs Jones .... have the day off.

3 There's **no law that requires** drivers to wear seat belts in my country.

   Drivers .... seat belts in my country.

4 I suppose **it's possible** her phone **isn't** working.

   I suppose her .... working.

5 **It's essential** that all competitors arrive on time.

   All competitors .... on time.

6 **Did you manage to** get a copy of this morning's paper?

   Were .... get a copy of this morning's paper?

7 **It's advisable** to have medical insurance when you travel.

   You .... medical insurance when you travel.

8 **It's not possible** for a person to lose so much weight so quickly.

   A person .... so much weight so quickly.

9 **It's likely** that Richard is on his way here now.

   Richard .... on his way here now.

10 **You are strictly prohibited** from smoking in any part of the building.

   You .... in any part of the building.

b Now complete the second sentence so that it has a similar meaning to the first sentence, using one of the phrases in the box. You don't have to use all the phrases in the box. Some of the phrases can be used more than once. You must complete the second sentence using between two and five words. Contractions count as two words.

Example: **There's a chance** the hurricane will hit northern towns tomorrow.
The hurricane <u>could hit</u> northern towns tomorrow.

Unit 3 Adjectives and adverbs

Language focus: uses of adjectives and adverbs; position and order of adjectives; forming adverbs from adjectives; position of adverbs

Exam focus: word formation and multiple-choice cloze questions

LEAD-IN

1 Look at the two sentences below and say what parts of speech are underlined.

a) Sheila's a heavy smoker but still attends **regular** <u>fitness classes</u>.
b) Sheila's a heavy smoker but still <u>attends</u> fitness classes **regularly**.

Now complete these general rules for adjectives and adverbs.

i) Adjectives are typically used with .... and adverbs are used with ....

ii) To form the adverb from the adjective we usually add ....

2 There are, however, various exceptions to the above two rules. Look at the three kinds of exception in the box and then read through the dictionary entries to find at least *two* more examples for each box.

---

a) With some words, the adverb and adjective are the same, e.g. **hard** (*he works hard*).

....

---

b) With some adjectives, as well as adding **-ly** to form the adverb, there is also a change in spelling, e.g. **probable – probably**.

....

---

c) Some verbs are followed by adjectives, not adverbs, e.g. **taste** (*it tastes funny*).

....

---

awful /ˈɔːfʊl/. **1** If you say that something **is awful**, you mean that it is **1.1** not very good or not very nice. EG *Isn't the weather awful?... Gas smells awful... The road is awful: narrow and bumpy... What an awful thing to say... ... married to that awful man.* **1.2** very unpleasant or very bad causing people to feel shock, fear, or sadness. EG *...an account of that awful war... My second husband had an awful death.*
2 If someone looks or feels **awful**, they look or feel ill. EG *I felt awful last night... God, he looks awful... My neck felt awful.* ADJ QUALIT ≈ terrible ≠ well

ADJ QUALIT ⇑ nasty ≈ dreadful ≈ wonderful ≈ horrific

fast /fɑːst/ **faster, fastest: fasts, fasting, fasted. 1** Something or someone that is **fast** moves, does ADJ QUALIT ≈ quick, swift something, or happens with great speed. EG *...a fast car... ...fast communications... Relationships today tend to change at a faster pace than ever before.* ▶ used as an adverb. EG *I ran as fast as I could... The music went faster and faster... News travels pretty fast... ...fast-flowing upland streams.* rapid ≈ slow

▶ ADV + VB

happy /ˈhæpɪ/, **happier, happiest. 1** Someone who is **happy** has feelings of pleasure, for example because something nice has happened or because they feel satisfied with their life. EG *I was happy to hear that you passed your exam... This will make the children happy.* ▶ used of a person's expression. EG *...a happy smile.* ◊ **happily.** EG *We laughed and chatted happily together.* ◊ **happiness.** EG *Money did not bring happiness.* ADJ QUALIT ⇑ content ≈ pleased ≠ sad

▶ ≈ cheerful
◊ ADV
◊ N UNCOUNT

late /leɪt/, **later, latest. 1 Late** is used to describe things that happen or are done near the end of a particular evening, day, year, etc. EG *She had stayed up late drinking vodka... ...in the late afternoon...* ADV. OR ADJ ≈ early

tragic /ˈtrædʒɪk/ **1** Something that is **tragic** is very sad because it involves death, suffering, or disaster. EG *The most tragic sight of all was the very young addicts... ...the tragic death of his elder brother Michael.* ◊ **tragically.** EG *He was tragically killed in a car crash.* ADJ QUALIT ⇑ distressing

◊ ADV WITH VB. OR ADV SEN

(from the *Collins COBUILD English Language Dictionary*)

REFERENCE

A *Uses of adjectives*

Adjectives are typically used:
1 before nouns
2 after certain verbs.

Adjectives before nouns

Where several adjectives are used in front of a noun there are clear rules about the order in which they should come.

1 Descriptive adjectives occur in the following order:
    size   age   shape   colour   origin   material

    *My cousin lives in a **large old Dutch** canal boat.*
    *The actor was wearing a **long red silk** scarf.*

2 Adjectives that express your opinion about something usually come before adjectives that describe the noun:

    *The necklace was made of **beautiful pink** glass.*

    If two 'opinion' adjectives are used, the more general one comes first.

    *We rented a **nice quiet** cottage by the sea.*

3 Adjectives used before nouns are only joined with **and** when the adjectives are of the same type, e.g. two colours.

    *The **black and white** rocket raced up into the clouds.*

1 **Read the sentences below and put the adjectives in front of the noun in the correct order.**

  1 The museum houses several (Japanese / stone / ancient) vases.
  2 The thieves used a (thin / long / wire) hook to open the door.
  3 My granddad kept his money in a (tin / funny / old / red) can.
  4 As he opened the cell door there was a (blinding / white) flash of light.
  5 My mother always says that I was a healthy baby with (large / blue / round) eyes.

Adjectives after certain verbs

1 After the following verbs we use adjectives, not adverbs:

appear	be	become	feel	look	seem	smell	sound	taste

*This apple **tastes funny**. Did you wash it?*
*I haven't had much sleep: that's why I **look so awful**.*
*The driver **became really angry** when I refused to move.*

Note, however, that some of these verbs can also be used with adverbs.

- **feel** with the meaning of 'touch' and in the phrase **feel well** to talk about health and illness.
  *The doctor **felt her injured arm carefully**.*
  *I really don't **feel well** – it must be the heat.*

- **look** with the meaning of 'study / focus the eyes on'.
  *The referee **looked quickly** at his watch.* (study)

- **appear** with the meaning of 'come into view'.
  *She **appeared suddenly** at the door.*

2 **Make, keep** and **find** are followed by adjectives when used in the following structure: 'verb + object + adjective'.
  *I **find it difficult** to believe that she didn't phone.*
  *The accident should **make him more careful** next time.*

B Uses of adverbs

1 With verbs:
  *The police **moved quickly** to stop a fight between the fans.*

2 Before adjectives:
  *The Divan Hotel has **reasonably priced** rooms.*

3 Before other adverbs:
  *My penfriend replied to my first letter **incredibly quickly**.*

4 Before prepositional phrases:
  *The plane shook and then went **completely out of control**.*

Forming adverbs

1 To form adverbs from adjectives we usually add **-ly** to the adjective: **slow – slowly, smooth – smoothly**.

2 **Good** is the only adjective with a completely irregular adverb: **well**.

3 For adjectives which already end in **-ly**, e.g. **friendly, cowardly, silly, ugly**, the adverb form is expressed by the phrase: **in a . . . way**.
  *The stranger asked **in a friendly way** if he could stay.*

4 Two other kinds of exception to the rule are adjectives which have the same adverb form and those where there is a spelling change to form the adverb (see table on next page).

2 Put the adjectives below into the correct box in the table. Then add the adverb form of each adjective. Two have already been done for you.

easy   straight   simple   good   ordinary   terrible
far · comic   hard   specific   fast   lucky

Change of spelling	*Irregular form*	*Adverb form same as adjective*
easy – easily		straight – straight

3 Now by looking at the *Change of spelling* box write two more rules like the one below.

1 With adjectives ending in 'y', the 'y' is replaced by 'i'.

2 ....

3 ....

Position of adverbs

1 Adverbs normally go after the verb.
He smokes heavily.

2 An adverb does not normally come between a verb and its direct object.
He studied the book carefully. (not: *He studied carefully the book.*)

3 If two or more adverbs are used, they usually come in the order:
manner   place   time
The plane landed smoothly right on time.
Didn't the team play well away from home last weekend?
She's been studying hard at home all year.

NOTE: The exceptions to this rule are verbs of motion – e.g. **go**, **come**, **arrive** – where the adverb of place tends to come before the adverb of manner.
She went upstairs quietly.

4 Complete each sentence with one of the words given at the end of the sentence. Two possible positions for the word are shown. Only one is correct.

1 The team plays .... at home ....   (good / well)

2 No one had said much but Paul seemed .... strangely ....
(quiet / quietly)

3 The police found .... his story .... to believe.
(hard / hardly)

4   We're looking for a .... quiet .... place to stay.
    (nice / nicely)

5   The exam looked .... at first .... but I'm sure I did well.
    (tough / toughly)

6   Most of our athletes ran .... this morning ....
    (superb / superbly)

7   I'm looking for a quiet, but .... located .... flat in the
    Heansley area.   (central / centrally)

8   The forest fire spread .... incredibly ....
    (quick / quickly)

COMMUNICATIVE PRACTICE

1 Rotten apples

Look at the unfinished sentences below and the lists of adjectives and adverbs that follow
them. With another student, work out which adjective or adverb could *not* be used to
complete each sentence. Then draw a line connecting all the words which do not fit (all
the 'rotten apples'). Then draw a second line parallel to the first one. For example: (far).

1 I found it . . .   (easy)   (strange)   (easily)   (far)

2 I felt . . .   (well)   (cheated)   (luckily)   (different)

3 It seemed . . .   (friendly)   (ordinarily)   (simple)   (cowardly)

4 I made it . . .   (comfortable)   (lost)   (quickly)   (eventually)

5 It sounds . . .   (frightened)   (fairly)   (hard)   (frightening)

6 I'll keep it . . .   (clean)   (quiet)   (tidily)   (temporarily)

7 I'll look . . .   (nice)   (thoroughly)   (personally)   (fashionably)

2 Palm reading

Look at the diagram and the table below. The diagram shows the lines of the palm and the table shows the name and significant features of each line. Working with another student, try to work out what each line can tell you. The first one has been done for you.

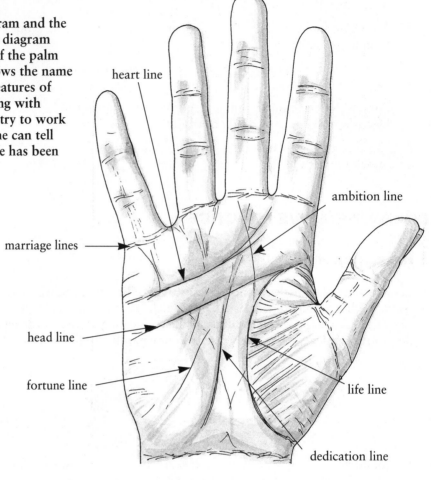

Name	Significant features	
Life line	A long line A break in the line	*indicates a long and healthy life.* *points to a period of serious illness.*
Dedication line	A long line . . . An unbroken line . . .	
Fortune line	The place where it begins . . .	
Head line	A long line . . .	
Marriage lines	The closeness to the heart line . . . The number of small lines . . .	
Heart line	A long curved line indicates . . . A deeply coloured line . . . The number of small lines coming from it . . .	
Ambition line	A long line . . . The place where it begins . . .	

Once you have checked your answers with your teacher, try reading each other's palms. You must read the right hand as shown in the diagram.

Example:

A: *You're going to have a long and healthy life, without being seriously ill.*

B: *Are you sure?*

A: *Yes. Look at how long your life line is – and there are no breaks in it.*

EXAM FOCUS

EXAM TIP 4

Three questions

There are three things you have to ask yourself when doing a word formation question:

a) what *part of speech* is needed in the gap?

b) will changing the word involve a *change of spelling*?

c) does a *prefix/suffix* need to be added?

1 Word formation

Read the text below and use the word given in capitals at the end of each line to form a word that fits in the space in the same line. There is an example at the beginning (0).

LineOne

Want to know what's on at your local jazz club, cinema, theatre or what's on TV this week?

Then it would be (0) inadvisable to miss out on LineOne.	ADVICE
From local to (1) .... listings to 24 hour news and sport, from a	NATION
comprehensive encyclopedia to an instant guide to (2) .... finance	PERSON
– all (3) .... updated. LineOne also offers on-line shopping, a	CONTINUE
(4) .... changing menu of fun activities for all the family and fast	CONSTANT
access to the wonders of the Internet, (5) .... e-mail.	INCLUDE
Jointly (6) .... by British Telecom and News International, LineOne	DEVELOP
is the most comprehensive on-line source of information about what's	
happening in the UK. It's easy to use, too. It's an (7) .... , self-contained	EXCLUDE
area on the Internet connected (8) .... to your Personal Computer, so	DIRECT
you can hop between LineOne areas (9) .... What's more, our unique	EASE
LineOne Intelligent Agent will (10) .... suggest new things to look at.	AUTOMATION
LineOne can help you get more from your PC and more out of life.	

(adapted from an advertisement for LineOne in *The Sunday Times Magazine*)

2 Multiple-choice cloze

Read the text below and think of the word which best fits each space. Use only *one* word
in each space.

Lightning strikes

The man who holds the record for being struck by lightning the most times is ex-park ranger,
Roy Sullivan. Mr Sullivan found lightning (1) .... to avoid: he was struck by it on
seven (2) .... occasions throughout his life, which were as (3) .... as
35 years apart.

 The first incident in 1942 was the only one where he was not (4) .... injured – he
only lost his big toenail. On all other occasions, he could (5) .... easily have lost
his life. In 1972 the 'human lightning conductor of Virginia', as he was known, had his hair
(6) .... on fire but was lucky enough to survive, only to lose all his new hair
in the same way a year later. It is hard to believe that he never lost his enthusiasm for
(7) .... hobbies and pursuits but when lightning struck for a record seventh
time in 1977 he was happily fishing, completely (8) .... that he was about to
enter *The Guinness Book of Records*. On this occasion he came (9) .... to death
because of severe chest and stomach burns. Roy Sullivan died in 1983 but was not killed
by lightning. He was (10) .... upset after being rejected in love and is said to have
taken his own life.

(adapted from *The Guinness Book of Records 1987* © Guinness Publishing Ltd 1986)

1	A difficult	B impractical	C necessary	D suitable
2	A various	B separate	C single	D apart
3	A long	B wide	C many	D far
4	A very	B highly	C seriously	D poorly
5	A well	B far	C quite	D much
6	A lit	B set	C put	D got
7	A outside	B outward	C outdoor	D outskirts
8	A unknown	B unbelievable	C unthinking	D unaware
9	A close	B next	C nearly	D almost
10	A strongly	B hardly	C deeply	D highly

Unit 4 The past

Language focus: uses of the past simple, past continuous, past perfect and past perfect
continuous; past tenses after special phrases

Exam focus: open cloze and error correction questions

LEAD-IN

Read these two short passages about the rainy season in South-East Asia and then complete
the task below.

Passage 1

The river was rising steadily when term ended. It was still possible to drive through the streets
of Kuala Hantu, but dwellers near the river's edge had taken to the roofs and the bazaar had had
to close down. Up-stream the rain thundered and soon, in time for Christmas, Kuala Hantu
would resound to the whip-lashings of the frenzied sky.

(adapted from Anthony Burgess, *The Long Day Wanes*)

Passage 2

Then, on a hot afternoon, we felt a fresh breeze hitting our faces. Small waves were beginning
to bump the boat. The wind had changed and the fish had begun their annual migration
northward. The monsoon that had been blowing constantly from the Indian Ocean from May to
September now gave way to the drier cooler monsoon from Mongolia. The rainy season was
over. An excited villager remarked that now the crabs and frogs would taste better.

(adapted from Thomas O'Neill, 'The Mekong River', *National Geographic*)

Mark the events mentioned in each passage on the time lines below, as in the example.

Passage 1

before	same time	after
	a	

end of term

a) the rising of the river   d) rain up-stream
b) moving to the roofs   e) lightning in Kuala Hantu
c) the closing of the bazaar

Passage 2

before	same time	after

one hot afternoon

a) waves around the boat   d) monsoon from the Indian Ocean
b) change in the wind   e) the villager's remark
c) migration of the fish   f) tastier crabs and frogs

REFERENCE

A The past simple

Form

Affirmative	*Negative*
I worked, etc.	I did not (didn't) work, etc.

Question	*Short answers*
Did you work?	Yes, I did. No, I didn't.

Some verbs have an irregular affirmative form. For a complete list of these see the back of the book.

Use

We use the past simple tense to talk about completed actions or habits in the past. We use it when some definite point or period in time is mentioned or understood.

*My husband and I **met in the last year of school**.*
*When I was at the market **this morning** I **saw** Pat.* (it's now afternoon)
*As a child I never **stayed** up later than nine o'clock.*

NOTE: In the last example, we could use the phrase **used to** to talk about past habit instead.

*As a child I **never used / didn't use to stay up** ...*

B The past continuous

Form

Affirmative	*Negative*
I was working, etc.	I was not (wasn't) working, etc.

Question	*Short answers*
Were you working?	Yes, I was. No, I wasn't.

Uses

1 We use the past continuous tense to talk about actions in progress in the past around a particular point in time.

 *I was probably **working** in the garden when you rang.*
 *My family **was living** in Germany at the time the Berlin Wall came down.*

 The actions are usually longer, rather than shorter, and we are not normally interested in when the past continuous action started or finished.

2 As well as talking about one general idea (a past action in progress) it is useful to think about the uses of the past continuous tense that are listed in the following exercise.

1 Look at the descriptions of uses in a–d and match them to each pair of example sentences in 1–4.

a) to provide background description or detail in a story
b) to describe actions which are interrupted
c) to talk about temporary situations in the past
d) to talk about two longer actions which happen at the same time

1 Sarah **was talking** to someone on the phone as I walked in.
 The film **was** just **getting** interesting when the picture went.

2 We both had friends who **were staying** in Spain that summer.
 I usually stacked the shelves but I **was working** at the check-out that week.

3 The child noticed that the man **was holding** an unusual stick.
 The rain **was beating** down outside and the children from the flat next door **were running** and **screaming** in the hallway.

4 I **was trying** to work while someone outside **was drilling**.
 The police didn't know that the murderer **was sitting** in jail accused of theft all the time they **were looking** for him.

2 Complete the story below by putting the verbs in brackets into either the past simple or past continuous tense.

A young English language student who (1) .... (spend) the summer in

Britain, (2) .... (decide) one day that he would like to visit a friend in another

town. Having just done a unit in his coursebook on 'public transport', he (3) ....

(think) it would be a good idea to take the train. He (4) .... (get) ready to

leave when he suddenly (5) .... (realise) that there was one important

phrase that the coursebook he (6) .... (use) at school had not taught him.

He (7) .... (take) out his dictionary and after a short search

(8) .... (find) the phrase 'return ticket'. Arriving at the train station, he

(9) .... (walk) boldly up to the ticket office and in his best English accent

said to the man who (10) .... (sit) at the desk: 'I'd like a return ticket,

please.' The man (11) .... (stare) at him for a moment questioningly and

then (12) .... (ask): 'Where to?' The student, who was used to his teacher

asking him such questions to check that he really (13) .... (understand) the

meaning of the words he (14) .... (use), looked confidently back at the man

and replied: 'Back here, of course.'

C *The past perfect*

Form

Affirmative	Negative
I had (I'd) worked, etc.	I had not (hadn't) worked, etc.

Question	Short answers
Had you worked?	Yes, I had. No, I hadn't.

Uses

1 When already talking about the past we use the past perfect to talk about an earlier past time.

   *His face was familiar. I **had met** him somewhere before.*
   *The hotel wasn't particularly good but I **had stayed** in many that were worse.*

2 We use the past perfect tense when one past action is closely connected to another to show which one happened first.

   *Wendy **hadn't left** the key so I climbed through a window.*

   This use is very common with time words and phrases such as:

when	before	after	by the time

   *Most of the guests **had left** by the time I got there.*
   *It began to rain just after the party **had started**.*

   NOTE: The past simple (not the past perfect) is used if one action is an immediate reaction to another.

   *When he **saw** the face at the window, he **fainted**.*
   *The child **stopped** crying as soon as she **caught** sight of her mother.*

D *The past perfect continuous*

Form

Affirmative	Negative
I had (I'd) been working, etc.	I had not (hadn't) been working, etc.

Question	Short answers
Had you been working?	Yes, I had. No, I hadn't.

Use

We use the past perfect continuous tense to talk about an action which had been in progress before another.

*I'd **been** quietly **reading** the paper before the train compartment filled up.*

Like the past continuous, it is used to talk about the longer, background events in a story.

*I'd **been visiting** doctors for several years with the same complaint before it was correctly diagnosed.*

E Past tenses after special phrases

The phrases below are followed by a special pattern of tenses: the past simple when there is a present focus to the sentence, and the past perfect when there is a past focus.

Present focus

*It's **time** we went/were going home.* (I think we should go.)
*I **wish** you didn't have to go.* (You have to go which makes me sad.)
*I'd **rather** we went together.* (I want us / I'd prefer to go together.)

Past focus

*I **wish** he hadn't come.* (I'm not happy that he came.)
*I'd **rather** we hadn't stayed so late.* (We stayed later than I wanted to.)
*If **only** you hadn't left.* (I'm unhappy that you left.)

3 Match sentences 1–6 to the explanations given in a–f.

1 It's time we had a holiday.
2 I wish we had had more time.
3 I wish we had a few more days.
4 I'd rather we stayed in a hotel.
5 If only we'd found a better hotel.
6 I'd rather we hadn't stayed so long.

a) This one is really dirty.
b) I really wanted to stay.
c) The campsite looks awful.
d) It was very expensive.
e) I'd really like to see some more sights.
f) We deserve a break.

4 Look at the following pairs of sentences and discuss the possible differences in meaning with another student.

Example:

a) When we got to the corner, Matthew waited.
   This means: 'Matthew was with us and when we got to the corner he stopped.'

b) When we got to the corner, Matthew was waiting.
   This means: 'Matthew was not with us. When we got to the corner he was there waiting for us.'

1 a) I was told that my friends hadn't waited for me.
   b) I was told that my friends hadn't been waiting for me.

2 a) The children went to bed when their parents got home.
   b) The children had gone to bed when their parents got home.

3 a) Mary didn't drive so she didn't have a car.
   b) Mary hadn't driven so she didn't have a car.

4 a) I argued with my wife when her parents came.
   b) I was arguing with my wife when her parents came.

5 a) Lucy hadn't been sleeping well at all before the interview.
   b) Lucy didn't sleep well at all before the interview.

6 a) I'd rather you didn't come with us.
   b) I'd rather you hadn't come with us.

COMMUNICATIVE PRACTICE

1 Short story bingo

Think of two *unusual* or *amusing* things that have happened to you in the past and think of how you can tell these stories. Look at the words in the bingo boxes below to help you remember, although you must not use these words in telling your short stories.

Now think about some of the vocabulary you will need to tell your stories.

Take it in turns to tell your stories to the class.

Below are two bingo cards. You will be given *one* of them to mark as your card. As you listen to the stories from other members of the class put an X in the box on your card if you hear an event or incident in a story that could be described by one of the phrases.

When you have a horizontal, vertical or diagonal line of three phrases, shout 'Bingo!'. You will then have to explain to the rest of the class which three incidents or events match the phrases you have marked.

The first person to get two correct lines is the winner.

A

Sweet revenge	Embarrassing moment	Strange coincidence
The wrong moment	Unexpected surprise	Unusual request
Lucky escape	Chance meeting	Misunderstanding

B

A total stranger	A stroke of good luck	Unique opportunity
Love at first sight	Lucky escape	A familiar face
Strange coincidence	Something peculiar	Chance meeting

2 Whose story?

Work with two other students. In your group decide upon a story to tell the rest of the class. The story has to be about something that has happened to *one* member of the group and it must be *true*.

When you have decided on a story, divide it up so that one person tells the beginning, another person the middle and the third person the end. Make sure every member of the group has all the facts they need to tell their part of the story.

When telling the story to the rest of the class, each member of the group must tell it as though it were his/her story (using the personal pronouns and possessive adjectives *I, we, my, our,* etc.). Tell the story as if you were really involved in what happened and try and give your listeners:

– the background situation / setting;
– important descriptive information about the characters / events;
– a sense of anticipation in waiting for the end.

After each story the rest of the class can ask *two* questions to any member of the group about the story. The rest of the class will then have to guess whose story it was.

EXAM FOCUS

1 Open cloze

Read the text below and think of the word which best fits each space. Use only *one* word in each space.

Adventure in China

At 15,000 feet on the Plateau of Tibet in China there was nowhere to hide. The snow flew like arrows. The Tibetan herder Meiga, who (1) .... forcing his horse through the storm, searched in vain for shelter. When visibility dropped to near zero all we could do (2) .... stop and bunch up the horses. Huddled together, heads bowed, we let the storm beat on us.

My goal was to travel the length of the Mekong, the world's twelfth longest river. To reach this place, I (3) .... travelled a thousand miles by old army jeep from Xining. Now, as we sheltered behind our horses, I wondered if we (4) .... have to turn back. Then the storm lifted, as suddenly as it (5) .... begun, leaving a bruised grey sky.

We rode another hour (6) .... coming to a solitary, cone-shaped hill. 'The holy mountain,' Meiga said. He reached into a saddlebag and pulled out a stack of coloured papers printed with Buddhist scripture. He shouted and flung the prayers high into the air and watched happily (7) .... the wind swept them away.

We rode behind the mountain and found a sheet of ice some 300 yards long – shaped

(8) .... an hourglass. Crouching down on the frozen surface, I

(9) .... hear below a trickle of water. It was the beginning notes of the

Mekong. Mike and I (10) .... become, as far as I can discover, the first

Western journalists to hear them.

(adapted from Thomas O'Neill, 'The Mekong River', *National Geographic*)

2 Error correction

a **The sentences below are not grammatically correct. They all contain one unnecessary word. Working with another student, identify the extra word and cross it out.**

1 I h̶a̶d̶ read the book *then* I saw the film.
2 I have told the police everything I know *last week*.
3 I was pushed *my way* through the door.
4 A lot of people had left *as* I got there.
5 The room was being painted *a long time ago*.

b **Now discuss with your partner how you could replace the words in italics with another word or phrase to make the sentences correct, without making any other changes.**

Example: (1) *I had read the book <u>before</u> I saw the film.*

c **Read the text below and look carefully at each line. Some of the lines are correct, and some have a word which should not be there. If a line is correct, put a tick by it. If a line has a word which should not be there, write the word at the end of the line. There are two examples at the beginning (0 and 00).**

A break-in

0	There are some things you don't forget quickly and coming home after a	✓
00	break-in is being one of them. I lived in a small flat in Bristol at the time	*being*
1	it had happened. As I opened the door I immediately knew that something	
2	was wrong because of the cold air coming from the broken window. The	
3	thieves, I suppose there were more than one, had been emptied everything	
4	onto the floor. My clothes, my books and the contents of all the drawers	
5	lay down in front of me as I walked in. They had taken lots of personal	
6	things that I wish after I had taken out with me that day. It is not that you	
7	mind losing little things like a radio or the small amount of cash you keep	
8	in the house but it is the way burglars often intrude into other people's	
9	lives. The thieves had gone through all the cupboards in the bedroom	
10	and were torn all my clothes. They even took my computer and all the	
11	disks, which meant I would had to spend weeks replacing my work. I	
12	reported the burglary to the police, who were very sympathetic, although	
13	they have informed me that there was not much chance that I would see	
14	my possessions again. I was used to be quite casual about security but I am	
15	more cautious now because I had hate to think of it happening to me again.	

Unit 5 **Articles and determiners**

Language focus: use of articles and determiners with countable and uncountable nouns
Exam focus: multiple-choice cloze and error correction questions

LEAD-IN

1 With another student, look at the words in the box below and decide whether they are likely to be used as *countable* nouns (with a plural form) or *uncountable* nouns (without a plural form). Write 'c' or 'un' next to each noun. Check your answers with another pair of students.

history	banking	world	gold bar	foreign currency
pottery	document	door	information	collection

2 The words and phrases in bold print in the text below are examples of how articles are used in English. Read the text and complete the 'Use of articles' table by matching at least one example to each rule.

The Bank of England Museum

(1) **The museum** is housed within the Bank of England itself, right at the heart of the City of London. It traces (2) **the history** of the Bank from its foundation by Royal Charter in 1694 to (3) t**he high-tech world** of (4) **modern banking**.

There are (5) **gold bars** dating from (6) **ancient times** to the modern market bar, coins and (7) **a unique collection** of banknotes, as well as many other items you might not expect to find – such as (8) **the Roman pottery and mosaics** uncovered when the Bank was rebuilt in the 1930s. On display are (9) **documents** relating to the Duchess of Marlborough and George Washington, both former customers of the Bank.

The Bank Stock Office, (10) **a late eighteenth-century banking hall** designed by the great English architect Sir John Soane, has been reconstructed and (11) **interactive videos** give visitors the opportunity of looking behind (12) **the doors** of the nation's central bank. (13) **Live news** and information about securities and (14) **foreign currency** is given at a dealing desk, which is identical to those in daily use in the Bank, and visitors can imagine themselves in the world of high finance.

(adapted from *Bank of England Museum: A Souvenir Guide*)

Use of articles

The

1 The is used with all nouns to talk about particular things when we say which one/ones we mean.   Examples: .... *2* ....
2 The is used with all nouns when the reader already knows the particular thing we are talking about, i.e. it has been mentioned before.   Example: ....

A / an

1 A / an is used with countable nouns when something is mentioned for the first time, when we mean '(there is) one'.   Example: ....
2 A / an is used with countable nouns to say what something or someone is, e.g. giving a definition of something, or saying what someone's profession is.   Example: ....

No article

1 No article is used with plural and uncountable nouns when we are talking about things in general, when we mean 'all'.   Examples: ....
2 No article is used with plural and uncountable nouns when something is mentioned in the text for the first time, when we mean '(there is / are) some'.   Examples: ....

REFERENCE

1 Discuss with another student whether the following statements are true or false. Then check your answers by reading Sections A and B below.

1 A singular countable noun, e.g. **boy**, can be used with no article.
2 The word **news** is used with a singular verb form.
3 In the following sentence both alternatives are grammatically correct: *I think I need a coffee / some coffee.*
4 We can talk about *a piece of advice* and *a piece of equipment*.

A *Countable nouns*

1 Countable nouns are those that have both a plural and singular form: things / persons that we can count.   *a policeman   two policemen   an armchair   several armchairs*

2 Singular countable nouns *must* be used with an article or similar word.

The headmaster needs a volunteer to help.
Every volunteer is welcome.

3 Plural countable nouns can be used with no article or with **some** or **any**.

Prices are unusually high this year.
Some books have gone missing from the library.
Aren't there any cheaper shoes left?

B Uncountable nouns

1 Uncountable nouns do not have a plural form and are always used with a singular form of the verb.

The weather has been really terrible lately.
The information isn't complete.

2 Uncountable nouns cannot be used with the indefinite article (**a / an**). They can be used with **some** and **any** or **no article**.

There isn't any milk left.
Bread and water are in short supply.

3 Sometimes, however, we do wish to talk about 'quantity' with uncountable nouns and then we have to use a special structure:

I need a bar of soap. (not 'a soap')
My family eats four loaves of bread a day. (not 'four breads')

4 The nouns below are uncountable in English but tend to be countable in other languages. All the nouns in bold print can be used with the phrase **a piece of**.

An important piece of equipment is missing.

advice	applause	damage	**equipment**	evidence	**furniture**	hair
harm	**information**	knowledge	lightning	**luggage**	**news**	
progress	proof	**research**	thunder	trouble		

5 Some nouns can be both countable and uncountable, e.g. materials and substances, depending on how we use them:

coffee	tea	beer	sugar	glass	paper	skin

Can I have a coffee? (a cup of . . .)
We've run out of coffee.

2 Complete each sentence below with a word from the box. (You won't need all the words.)

skin	assistant	idea	beer	equipment
news	tool	advice	customer	reports

1 You're working too hard. You need a reliable ....

2 Haven't you got rough .... ?

3 I'm afraid we can't serve .... before six o'clock.

4 .... of the situation in Africa get worse each day.

5 You need a different .... to do the job properly.

6 Contact an employment agency to get an .... about how much extra staff will cost.

7 I've heard a piece of .... that might interest you.

8 You can't expect to satisfy every .... all the time.

3 Complete the sentences below by choosing the correct alternative of the two given in brackets. Then check your answers by reading through Sections C and D.

(The line —— means 'no article'.)

1 The book contained very .... useful information.   (few / little)

2 .... French have a great football team at the moment.   (—— / The)

3 Did Beethoven ever compose for .... guitar?   (a / the)

4 .... prices fell during the second half of the year.   (Most / Less)

5 I'm afraid there isn't really .... advice I can give.   (much / another)

6 .... cigarettes aren't as popular as they used to be.   (—— / The)

C Articles

1 **The** is used with all nouns:

   a when the listener/reader already knows the person / thing we are talking about.
   *I can't give you **the five pounds** back.*

   b when we say exactly which person / thing we mean.
   ***The** glass you just gave me is cracked.*
   ***The** famous actress **Cher** was there.*

   c when there is only one of the thing we are talking about.
   ***The** environment is in great danger.*

   d and with these categories of noun to talk about the thing in general:
   musical instruments   animals   plants   inventions   nationalities.
   *I play **the guitar** quite well.*
   ***The** Spanish make the best salads.*

2 **A / an** is used with singular countable nouns:

   a when mentioning something / someone for the first time.
   *The museum also has **a rare sculpture**.*

   b to say what someone / something is.
   *My uncle is **a teacher**.*

c to talk about a person / thing in general.
A car is no longer considered a luxury.

3 No article is used with plural and uncountable nouns:

a when we mention the thing / things for the first time.
Food and drinks will be served later.

b when we talk about the thing / things in general.
Life in the developing world is tough.
Modern cars last five to ten years.

D Determiners

1 The following determiners are all used with singular countable nouns. Those in bold print can *only* be used with singular countable nouns.

a / an	another	any	each	either	every	neither	no

Every member was given a free pass.

2 The following determiners are all used with plural countable nouns. Those in bold print can *only* be used with plural countable nouns.

all	any	**both**	enough	few	fewer	many
more	most	no	**other**	**several**	some	

Several guests arrived after the speeches.

3 The following determiners are all used with uncountable nouns. Those in bold print can *only* be used with uncountable nouns.

all	any	enough	**less**	**little**	more	most	**much**	no	some

The speakers were given very little time.

4 Many is used with plural countable nouns, **much** with uncountable nouns.
There aren't many lakes in Greece.
How much aid had already reached the area?

But they are only used in questions and negative statements. In affirmative statements we use **a lot of**.
A lot of equipment was damaged by the fire.

5 Little / a little are used with uncountable nouns.
Little money has been given so far. (not much)
A little money would help a lot. (some)

6 Few / a few are used with plural countable nouns.
Very few countries grow all their own food. (not many)
A few people have already been informed. (some)

COMMUNICATIVE PRACTICE

1 Which one fits?

With another student look at the types of food and drink in the box and decide which words are used as uncountable nouns and which ones as countable nouns when talking about the food and drink in general.

Example: *Potato is a countable noun.*

potato   cheese   chocolate   tea   egg   coffee

Write the words in the table below. (The first one has been done for you.)

Now decide which one of these types of food and drink fits all the categories below. There is *only one* right answer.

	Can affect your sleep	*Can harm your teeth*	*Can make you more excitable or alert*	*It, or its main ingredient, comes from the southern hemisphere*	*Can be counted like soap*
potatoes					
....					
....					
....					
....					
....					

2 What's missing?

Look at the cartoons. Something is missing from each one. With another student read the caption that goes with each cartoon and try and work out what the missing parts of the picture might be.

1

'OK, kids, bedtime.'

2

'How's the article on recycling going?'

3

4

5

'Oh, thank God – I hate to drink alone!'

6

'I'm sorry, but I think I've forgotten your name.'

EXAM FOCUS

EXAM TIP 5

Spotting the grammar point

In some of the questions in the multiple-choice cloze, getting the answer right depends on spotting the grammar point in the text that will help you to eliminate most, if not all, of the wrong answers. In questions involving *nouns* you should first spot whether you are dealing with a countable or uncountable noun.

1 Multiple-choice cloze

The advertisement below is from an airline magazine. First decide whether the noun you are given or are looking for is countable (c) or uncountable (un). Then decide which answer A, B, C or D best fits each space.

Join our team

Are you enjoying your flight with us? Then why not think about joining us? We are a friendly company, proud of the service we offer passengers on (1) .... our scheduled and charter flights. We select our cabin crew with great (2) .... – you wouldn't be just a number, you would be an important (3) .... of our team.

Minimum requirements:

You must be 19 to 34 years old and 160 cm to 187 cm tall (with weight in proportion to height). You must have achieved a good (4) .... of education, be capable of swimming 23 metres and be medically fit.

Here are some typical questions that our cabin crew are asked:

What hours do you work? Very varied. We do shift (5) .... which involves early morning, afternoon or night flights.

What is the best thing about the job? Every day is different and individual. A new day, a new destination. We never take our work home with us and when the flight lands it is the end of that day and the (6) .... flight will be totally different and unrelated.

What do you expect to earn? A very respectable (7) .... There's a flying allowance for the duration of your day, allowances for languages, nursing skills and commission.

What training is needed? Five intensive weeks. It involves cabin service, (8) .... (including fire fighting, aircraft evacuation and life raft skills) and first aid. (9) .... of the training is in the classroom; however, time is spent in our mock aircraft cabin at head office in Luton.

Do you need any personal qualities? You need to be calm and approachable and enjoy working with the (10) ....

(adapted from Monarch Airlines' *Inflight* magazine)

		A	B	C	D
1	(c/un)	A either	B each	C both	D any
2	(c/un)	A search	B care	C time	D examination
3	(c/un)	A piece	B part	C item	D single
4	(c/un)	A evidence	B proof	C achievement	D standard
5	(c/un)	A job	B work	C hour	D employment
6	(c/un)	A next	B other	C one	D every
7	(c/un)	A pay	B earning	C salary	D money
8	(c/un)	A safety	B disaster	C accident	D emergency
9	(c/un)	A Majority	B More	C Most	D Several
10	(c/un)	A passenger	B tourist	C people	D public

EXAM TIP 6

Understanding the context

When you do the error correction task in Part 4, it's important to think about the context carefully. What may look like correct English at first, may not be correct in *this* context. The use of articles, for example, may depend on whether something has been mentioned before. Remember that we often don't use articles when we mean 'some' or 'all'.

2 Error correction

a Read the text below and look carefully at each line. Some of the lines are correct and some have a word which should not be there. If a line is correct, put a tick by it. If a line has a word which should not be there, write the word at the end of the line. There are two examples at the beginning (0 and 00).

A visit to Spain

0   The first time I visited Spain I couldn't speak a word of the Spanish. My   *the*

00 money ran out after a few weeks so I had to come up with a quick way of   ✓

1   making the cash if I was going to stay in the country. I had thought that I

2   could play the guitar, but I soon realised that in the home of the classical

3   guitar my busking skills would not be in demand! I had one luggage I could sell

4   but the money from that would only last me for a few another days. But, I

5   got lucky. Few foreigners get the chance to work on a Spanish farm in winter,

6   although there are some jobs during harvest time, but I did. By the chance

7   I met Luis working in a street market. He was selling all fruit and vegetables

8   on his father's stall. He was my age and soon noticed that I was an English.

9   He said it was because the English always look uncomfortable in the bustle

10 of the market and never get served first in a crowd of the people. Luis had

11 wanted to go to England for some time to improve his English but hadn't been

12 able to afford it. When he heard I needed somewhere to stay he said I

13 could stay with his family and help out with jobs like cleaning few farming

14 equipment. I eagerly accepted. The both his parents were wonderful to me

15 and I loved life on the farm. I had a little time to learn Spanish though

    because Luis spoke English all the time!

b The ten mistakes in lines 1–15 of the text above are all connected with articles and determiners. Working with a partner, look back at each mistake in context. Can you explain why the errors occurred?

Unit 6 Dependent prepositions

> *Language focus:* dependent prepositions after adjectives and verbs; dependent
> prepositions and sentence patterns
>
> *Exam focus:* open cloze and multiple-choice cloze questions

LEAD-IN

1 Albert is a complex person with many different
characteristics. These are shown in the maze of
his mind below, with positive characteristics on
the left and negative ones on the right. However,
the prepositions in these descriptions have all been
missed out, and where they are missing there are
gaps in the walls of the maze.

Working in a group, start in the middle of the maze and try to get out through the
positive side by choosing the correct prepositions. For example, 'good at hiding feelings'
will allow you to go through that gap. You only need to go through one gap in each wall.

Write down the prepositions you choose, and when you have found a way out, tell your
teacher. If your prepositions are all correct, you have won. If not, you must wait to try
again until another group has checked their prepositions with the teacher.

When one group has won, do the same with the negative side of the maze.

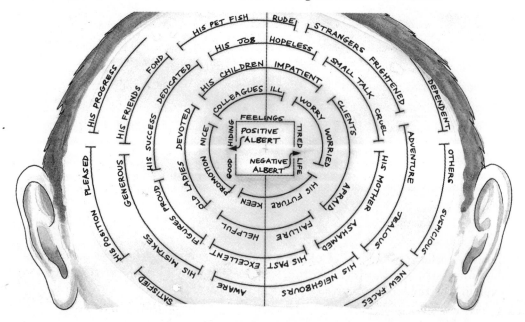

2 Look back at the maze and write in the box below any adjectives to do with *ability* (how good/bad someone is).

Look back at the maze and write in the box below any adjectives to do with *people's behaviour towards things / other people.*

Which preposition do these adjectives take?

REFERENCE

A *Dependent prepositions after adjectives*

Complete the second example in each box so that it is a true statement about yourself.

1 **At** is used after adjectives of ability:
awful   bad   excellent   good   great   terrible   useless

*My son's not so **good at** maths.*
I'm really
....

2 **To** and **of** are used with adjectives describing behaviour:
cruel   friendly   helpful   kind   nasty   nice   offensive   polite   rude

To refers to the object of the action:
*She was **rude to** her father.*
.... *to me.*

Of in phrases with an impersonal subject (**it/that**):
*It/that was really **kind of** you.*

3 **About** and **with** are used with adjectives describing reactions to people/events:
concerned   embarrassed   positive   worried   **about** something / someone

*Our teacher is **concerned about** our slow progress.*
....

bored   disgusted   impressed   patient   **with** somebody / something

*He's very **patient with** the children.*
....

angry   annoyed   furious   upset   **with** somebody / **about** something

*Eva got **upset with** me for not calling.*
....

disappointed   happy   pleased   **with** somebody / **about** an event / **with** a situation
*I'm not **pleased with** the way my work is going.*
*He's very **happy about** being selected to play on Saturday.*
I'm really not ....

---

4 **Of** is used with certain adjectives describing more lasting feelings:
afraid   ashamed   fond   frightened   jealous   suspicious   tired   wary
*Who's the child so **afraid of**?*
I've never ....

---

5 NOTE: Sometimes words such as **frightened, worried, upset** and **embarrassed** are used as past participle forms. When used in a passive construction they will be followed by the preposition **by**.
*My cousin is **frightened of** spiders.* (always)
*My cousin was **frightened by** a spider running across the floor.* (this spider frightened him)

B *Dependent prepositions after verbs*

Read the information in the boxes below and complete the second sentence in each box to make a true statement about you and the FCE exam. This could be about preparing for or sitting the exam, or about getting the results.

---

1 **At** is used after certain verbs to show the object of attention:
aim   fire   laugh   look   point   scream   shout   smile   stare
throw   whistle   yell
*Our neighbour often **stares at** me through the window.*
....

---

2 **For** is used after certain verbs to introduce the purpose of the action:
apologise   hope   look   long   pray   search   wait
*We're **hoping for** better weather this time.*

It is also used with certain transitive verbs this way:
ask   blame   forgive   prepare
*The rest of the team **blamed me for** the mistake.*
*She's never **forgiven me for** not telling her.*
....

---

3 **About** is used after certain verbs of speech to introduce the topic:
ask   complain   explain   lie   talk   tell   warn   wonder   write
*Was the driver **lying about** his address?*
....

4 **To** is used after certain verbs of speech to introduce other people involved:
apologise   explain   listen   speak   suggest   talk   write
*Has your boss **apologised to** you yet?*

....

5 **On** is used after certain verbs to introduce the object of the action:
check   concentrate   count   depend   insist   rely
*We can't **rely on** my parents coming to get us.*
In writing the essays ....

6 **From** is used after certain verbs which have the meaning of stopping something:
discourage   dissuade   keep   prevent   stop
*The guards **prevented me from** leaving the room.*
Nothing ....

C *Dependent prepositions and sentence patterns*

1 After a dependent preposition we use an **-ing** verb form.
*My brother is afraid **of people laughing** at him.*
*Aren't our neighbours talking **about moving** abroad?*

But with some adjectives we can drop the preposition and use an infinitive instead.
*She's **afraid to go** out alone.*

We also use an infinitive when an adjective is used with **too**.
*The child was **too embarrassed to** perform.*

2 The object pronoun relating to a following verb comes between the dependent preposition and the **-ing** form.
*Aren't you bored **with him talking** about himself?*

3 The negatives **not** and **never** also come between the dependent preposition and the **-ing** form.
*The patient apologised **for not being** on time.*

4 When **to** is a dependent preposition it is followed by an **-ing** form as in the following words / phrases:

look forward to	be opposed to	get/be used to	dedicated to
prefer . . . to	admit to	object to	

*I **prefer getting** up early **to staying** on late at work.*
*My son's never really been **dedicated to becoming** a doctor.*
(See Unit 8 for dependent prepositions and relative clauses.)

1 Match the beginnings of the questions on the left to the ends of the questions on the right.

1 Don't you think we should complain	a) to see anyone?
2 Why don't you explain	b) you for what happened?
3 Shouldn't you concentrate	c) for the delay?
4 Won't she be too upset	d) it to her?
5 Aren't you tired	e) on getting better, rather than work?
6 Didn't Kim apologise	f) with your results?
7 Does Keith blame	g) of not having any free time?
8 Aren't you pleased	h) to them about having to wait?
9 Hasn't he already asked	i) to us doing overtime?
10 Do you think they'll object	j) you for some money?

COMMUNICATIVE PRACTICE

1 How did you feel?

Imagine yourself in two of the situations below. Write about how you felt in each one using at least two or three of the adjectives from the Lead-in and Reference sections.

Example: (1) *It was really wrong of him to do that. I felt so embarrassed about it at the time and really annoyed with him afterwards. He was playing with people's feelings and being cruel to both of us.*

1 A friend arranged a blind date for you with someone twice (or half) your age.
2 You were caught looking at someone else's answer paper during an exam.
3 On a walk through a forest you got separated from the rest of the group.
4 In a busy department store you were wrongly accused of shoplifting by a store detective.
5 Your friends laughed at you when you told them that you had applied for a much better job.
6 You went out one night with a group of friends and you ended up buying most of the drinks.
7 You went to see your boss about a personal problem and he/she said that he/she didn't have time to discuss it.
8 You were elected student of the year by teachers and had to give a speech to the whole school.

Then show your descriptions to two other students and see if they can guess which situations you have written about. Do not describe what happened, only how people reacted and how you felt.

Discuss how the two other students in your group felt in their imaginary situations. Would you feel the same way?

2 A murder mystery

Lady Stephanie Chattsworth died from kissing a letter written with poisoned ink. Read
the information below about Lady Stephanie and the people suspected of her murder.
Then, using the verbs on the arrows below, discuss with another student how the
characters felt about each other and who might have murdered Lady Stephanie.

For example, with *forgave* on the arrow from Lord Chattsworth to Lady Stephanie you
could say, 'Lord Chattsworth forgave his wife for her affair with the butler.'

Lady Stephanie Chattsworth
was a very attractive
forty-year-old woman.
She was very fond of her
husband, Lord Chattsworth,
but fell madly in love with
the butler at Chattsworth
Manor, Craig Walker.
She died after kissing the
poisoned picture of a red rose.

forgave

explained

was convinced   disapproved

depended

was lying

objected

was preventing

blamed

hated

Lord Chattsworth is a seventy-
year-old millionaire. He was
deeply upset by his wife's
affair with the butler, Craig
Walker, and has sacked Mr
Walker.

Suzanne Chattsworth is Lord
Chattsworth's only daughter.
Her mother, the first Lady
Chattsworth, died three years
ago, and she did not want her
father to marry again. She loves
the life of high society and spends
all her time, and a lot of money,
on going to parties.

was relying

longed

Craig Walker is a handsome
young man who had never
worked as a butler before
coming to Chattsworth Manor.
It was Lord Chattsworth's
daughter, Suzanne, who
encouraged her father to
employ him. Now he has lost
his job he regrets the affair
with Stephanie.

EXAM FOCUS

1 Open cloze

a **Read the text below and think of the preposition which best fits each space. Use only** *one* **preposition in each space.**

It was getting very late and she was worried (1) .... Steve. He had told her

something (2) .... a man he would have to wait (3) .... but had rushed

out of the door before she could ask any more. You could usually rely (4) ....

Steve to be frank and honest but he had changed of late and Annie objected (5) ....

him being so secretive. Something or someone was stopping him (6) .... coming

clean. She was tired (7) .... all the pretence and promised herself that she would

ask him (8) .... a thorough explanation as soon as he walked through the door.

b **Read the text below and think of the word which best fits each space. Use only** *one* **word in each space. You will need to use various types of words (verbs, prepositions, negatives, etc.) but all the missing words relate in some way to the grammar covered in this unit.**

Thais are naturally friendly people and will want to make you feel at home. There are a few

basic rules you should observe, however. Do not point your feet directly (1) .... a

Thai – it is deeply offensive (2) .... them. Always dress discreetly in a *wat* [temple]

and remember that you will not be forgiven lightly for (3) .... taking off your shoes.

Thais are now (4) .... to seeing tourists bathe topless but nude bathing is definitely

unacceptable. Thais greet each other (5) .... a palms-together gesture; if you do

likewise you will give considerable pleasure. Thais are curious people, so will ask you

questions that westerners would not normally ask – (6) .... your salary, for example.

Do not be offended (7) .... this. It is normal to bargain in Thailand and Thais will not

get upset about you (8) .... for money off – about 15–20 per cent. Lastly, enjoy

yourself, that's a very Thai thing to do!

(adapted from Christine Osborne, *Essential Thailand*)

2 Multiple-choice cloze

Read the text below and decide which answer A, B, C or D best fits each space.

Learn English in Britain

Over 600,000 students come to Britain each year to learn English and immerse themselves (1) .... a complete cultural experience. It's a great place to study offering many attractions which cannot be found anywhere else. Why not (2) .... your stay with visits to other European countries which can be easily (3) .... from Britain?

We have a variety of exciting places in which to study – cosmopolitan cities, traditional centres of learning, coastal resorts, beautiful historic towns. The choice is yours.

Scotland: Tartan, bagpipes, whisky, mountains and islands are just some of the things for which Scotland is (4) .... Visitors are (5) .... to Scotland's spectacular colourful scenery. The Scottish Borders with green rolling countryside, winding rivers and woodlands are likely to (6) .... to walkers. The Highlands is an area of wild beauty (7) .... in wildlife and rare plants, with heather covered moorlands and fast flowing rivers.

Northumbria: Northumbria boasts more castles and ruins than any other English region. Along the entire width of northern England (8) .... Hadrian's Wall, built by the Romans to (9) .... the Scots from crossing the border. Northumbria also has miles of beautiful sandy beaches.

London: The capital offers superb shopping; Oxford Street, Regent Street and Knightsbridge are all known (10) .... their famous stores. If you are looking (11) .... unusual items, Harrods in Knightsbridge boasts that it can order anything in the world. For those (12) .... in sports, there's tennis at Wimbledon, cricket at Lords and rugby at Twickenham as well as many other well known events.

(adapted from ARELS, *Learn English in Britain*)

1	A	of	B	in	C	at	D for
2	A	join	B	divide	C	combine	D concentrate
3	A	got	B	passed	C	travelled	D reached
4	A	famous	B	worthy	C	attractive	D pleasant
5	A	pleased	B	attracted	C	enthused	D delighted
6	A	search	B	attract	C	appeal	D fascinate
7	A	full	B	excellent	C	fond	D rich
8	A	passes	B	starts	C	runs	D flows
9	A	prevent	B	suspend	C	refuse	D defend
10	A	as	B	by	C	for	D with
11	A	around	B	at	C	over	D for
12	A	good	B	interested	C	occupied	D fond

Unit 7 The present perfect simple and continuous tenses

> *Language focus:* uses of the present perfect simple tense; contrast with the past simple tense; uses of the present perfect continuous tense
>
> *Exam focus:* key-word transformation and error correction questions

LEAD-IN

1 The texts below show three different uses of the present perfect simple tense. Read the texts and note the circled perfect tenses. Then look at the four statements which follow. Three of them accurately describe the use of the perfect tense in the texts; one is false. Tick the three true statements for each use.

Use 1

THE PARENTS of a teenager who has stolen 400 cars last night pleaded for him to be given a tougher sentence if he does it once more.

They fear he might kill someone if he carries on with his life of crime, and say locking him up is the only way to stop him.

The 15-year-old tearaway – who (has so far taken) cars worth more than £3 million – is due to be released in a few weeks after serving half his youth custody term.

(from the *Daily Mail*)

The present perfect simple tense is used here to talk about

A   a situation which began in the past.
B   a situation which continues up to the present.
C   a situation which finished some time ago.
D   a period of time rather than a specific point in time.

Use 2

The present perfect simple tense is used here to talk about

A   a recent past action.
B   exactly when the action happened.
C   an action the speaker/writer believes to be news.
D   a past action which has some present effect or result.

Use 3

Rosamund Richardson is the author of several books, and presenter of BBC TV's 'Discovering Patchwork' and co-presenter of BBC TV's 'Discovering Hedgerows'. She has also done a short cookery series for BBC East and a series on the uses of herbs for Anglia Television. She has been a regular contributor to BBC Radio Cambridgeshire.

(from Rosamund Richardson, *Vegetarian Meals*)

The present perfect simple tense is used here to talk about

A an action/event which has finished.
B exactly when the action happened.
C an action which happened at some time before now.
D past experience connected to what we are talking about now.

2 From what you have seen in Task 1, which two of these three statements are true of all uses of the present perfect simple tense?

1 The present perfect simple can only be used to talk about the recent past.
2 The present perfect simple is not used to talk about exactly when a past event happened.
3 The present perfect simple is used to talk about past events which have some connection with the present.

REFERENCE

A *The present perfect simple*

Form

Affirmative	*Negative*
I have (I've) decided, etc.	I have not (haven't) decided, etc.
Question	*Short answers*
Have you decided?	Yes, I have. No, I haven't.

Uses

1 The present perfect simple is used to talk about an action which began in the past and continues up to the present.
I've had this pain in my back all week.
The resort has changed a lot in recent years.
It hasn't rained here for weeks.

The time expressions in box 1 are commonly used with this meaning of the present perfect simple.

Box 1

all (day)	for ages	for (two) years	How long . . . ?	lately	so far
over the (past few weeks)	recently	since (Tuesday)	up to now		

2 For / since / ago

For and **since** are used to talk about the time between the start of a situation and now. The situation is one that continues up to the moment of speaking / writing.

For is used to talk about the length or period of time, i.e. the number of hours / days. **Since** is used to talk about the period of time from the point at which it began.

Ago is used to talk about the time at which a situation began in the past. The past simple is used.

Example:

A: *Your fax arrived **two days ago**.*
B: *You mean that you've had it **for two days** and haven't replied?*
A: *I'm sorry, but I haven't been to the office **since Monday** and I've only just seen it.*

1 Complete the following sentences with either the present perfect simple or the past simple so that they are true about yourself.

1 I have lived ....

2 .... recently.

3 I've not been ....

4 .... for a long time.

5 .... some time ago.

3 The present perfect simple is used when a past action has some present effect or result.
*My watch **has stopped**.* (It might be later than we think.)
***Has** anyone **seen** my car keys?* (If you have, I can leave.)

NOTE: If we use a definite past time expression, as in box 2, the past simple tense must be used as there is no longer any idea of present effect. (See Unit 4 for more information about the past simple.)

Box 2

(hours) ago	at (six)	before (Tuesday)	during (the holiday)	earlier
in (May)	last (week)	on (Monday)	the other day	this (morning)

Compare the two responses in these two dialogues:

A: *I've lost my wallet.*
B: *Don't panic. It must be here somewhere.*

B: *Have you had a good day?*
A: *No, I lost my wallet this morning.*

4 We use the present perfect simple to talk about things that have or haven't happened at some time before the time of speaking / writing but we do not say exactly when.

Has anyone in the class been to the museum before?
I've passed my driving test but I'm waiting for my licence.

The time expressions in box 3 are commonly used with this meaning of the present perfect simple.

Box 3

| mid-position adverbs: already | always | ever | never | still |
| *end-position adverbs / adverbial phrases*: before | | several times | | yet |

NOTE: **Still** is rather unusual in that it can also come before the whole verb phrase.

2 Put the words in the jumbled sentences below into the correct order. Think carefully about the position of the time adverb.

1 their / once / has / before / invaded / army

....

2 teacher / has / our / not / history / taught / always

....

3 you / been / the / to / have / yet / bank / ?

....

4 still / has / postman / not / the / come

....

5 they / never / been / trouble / have / before / in

....

6 police / have / the / already / not / twice / here / been / ?

....

B *The present perfect continuous*

Form

Affirmative	*Negative*
I have (I've) been working, etc.	I have not (haven't) been working, etc.

Question	*Short answers*
Have you been working?	Yes, I have. No, I haven't.

Uses

The uses of the present perfect continuous are best seen in comparison with the uses of the present perfect simple.

Present perfect continuous	*Present perfect simple*
Using the present perfect continuous may mean that the action is not finished. *We've been painting the house but still have a lot to do.*	The present perfect simple is used when the action or situation is finished. *We've painted the whole house both inside and out.*
The present perfect continuous is used to talk about the length of time an activity has been in progress. *How long have you been teaching?*	The present perfect simple is used to talk about the result of an activity, e.g. when talking about quantities or distances. *How many schools have you taught in?*
The present perfect continuous is used to talk about temporary situations. *The shop hasn't been making any money recently.*	The present perfect simple is used to talk about situations that are long-lasting or permanent. *The shop has never made any money.*
The present perfect continuous is often used when the effects of an action are still visible. *Look. It's been raining.*	The present perfect simple is used to talk about the start or ending of an action. *Has it stopped raining yet?*

NOTE: The present perfect continuous is often used with the time adverbs in Box 1 but *never* with those in Boxes 2 and 3.

3 Complete the following short dialogues with the questions which produced B's responses.

1 A: How long .... ?

   B: Since last month at this school and two years at an English language college in Japan before that.

2 A: How much .... ?

   B: About forty-five pounds so far, but I've still got quite a bit left.

3 A: What have .... ?

   B: Mending the car again. That's why I look such a mess.

4 A: .... Don yet?

   B: Yes, I saw him this morning. He looks fine.

5 A: .... here all your life?

   B: No. I moved here about four years ago.

6 A: Have you .... ?

   B: No, not long. I had my first cigarette when I was eighteen.

COMMUNICATIVE PRACTICE

1 Messages around the house

Look at the picture of the house below and read the three messages. Where do you think they were left? Mark the places on the picture.

Why are present perfect tenses used in messages like this?

Now write a similar message about a particular object in the picture of the house but do not name it. Read your message and get the rest of the class to guess what it is.

2 Since then

Make notes about yourself four years ago under the various headings in the table below.

	Four years ago	*Since then*
Address:		
Appearance:		
Holidays:		
Hobbies:		
Taste in music:		
Ambitions:		
Worries:		

Ask another student questions about the information in their box to find out more about them four years ago and since then.

Example:

A: *Where did you go on holiday four years ago?*
B: *I went to Spain with my family.*
A: *Have you been back there since then?*
B: *Yes, we've been going every year since then but we always go to a different resort.*

Then tell another pair of students about your partner.

3 Three in a row

Read the sentences below and, with another student, complete each one with three adverbs or adverbial phrases from the grid. Find three that occur in a horizontal, vertical or diagonal row.

all month	all week	just	already	recently
the other day	yet	for ages	ever	several times
before Christmas	before	in May	lately	twice
during the lesson	this week	last	still	never

Example: *Has he done the cleaning* ~~before~~ / yet / this week *?*

1 Our neighbours have .... moved in next door.

2 I saw the teacher really lose his temper ....

3 That student .... came to class after her skiing accident.

4 We've been having problems with our car ....

5 Our boss has had the car repaired ....

EXAM FOCUS

1 Key-word transformation

a Complete the second sentence so that it has a similar meaning to the first sentence, using one of the two key-words given (only one will help you to write the sentence correctly). You must use between two and five words, including the key-word. Note: In this part of the exam you are only given *one* key-word.

Example: The last time I saw her was at Peter's party.
I *haven't seen her since* Peter's party.   **after / since**

Contractions such as **haven't** count as two words. This means that, in the example above, *five* words have been used, the maximum number allowed.

1 I haven't been here before.

   It's the .... here.   **time / since**

2 It's ages since my sister was last here.

   My sister .... ages.   **isn't / hasn't**

3 My father began smoking when he was eighteen.

   My father has .... he was eighteen.   **since / when**

4 He started working here three months ago.

   He .... three months.   **since / for**

5 When did he start playing for United?

   How .... for United?   **played / playing**

6 I haven't spoken to her for two weeks.

   The .... to her was two weeks ago.   **last / previous**

7 He fell ill on Friday morning.

   He .... Friday morning.   **was / has**

8 He began work on the book two months ago.

   He .... on the book for two months.   **worked / working**

EXAM TIP 8

Every sentence has a verb

All sentences have verbs, and in the key-word transformation questions in Part 3 it will often be the verb phrase that you have to change in some way. Always check that you have made all the necessary changes.

Example: I'm sure he forgot about the appointment.
He *must have forgotten about* the appointment.   *must*

b Working with another student decide which key-word you will need from the box below to complete the second sentence so that it has a similar meaning to the first. Then complete the sentences. You must use between two and five words, including the key-word.

at   first   get   became   never   since

1 He hasn't had a holiday for years.

It's .... had a holiday in years.

2 The last time it rained here was in May.

It .... May.

3 He has been President for six months now.

Six months .... President.

4 How long have they been married?

When .... married?

5 It's the first time he has failed an exam.

He .... an exam before.

6 I haven't seen Jane since her wedding.

The last time .... her wedding.

EXAM TIP 9

Errors and extra words

In the error correction task in Part 4 you have to read the text carefully to look for words which should not be there – words which do not fit in the context of the text. You are not looking for words that *could* be removed, only those which *must* be removed because they are incorrect in terms of grammar or meaning.

'YOU HAVE A LOVELY HAIR'

2 Error correction

a Read the text below and look carefully at each line. Some of the lines are correct and some have a word which should not be there. If a line is correct, put a tick by it. If a line has a word which should not be there, write the word at the end of the line. There are two examples at the beginning (0 and 00).

> Dear John,
>
> 0 It has been a long time since I wrote to you last. I should have ✓
>
> 00 written sooner but I've been such busy with the house and haven't   such
>
> 1 had time to put pen to paper. As you can see from the address above,
>
> 2 I have now moved into the new house. I've been making unpacking
>
> 3 since I arrived and still haven't finished yet. It's been hectic because
>
> 4 I have moved in at the weekend and began painting on Tuesday. I
>
> 5 have not been at work for the past few days because I am determined
>
> 6 to get everything ready by summer. I've been really busy all past week
>
> 7 trying to get things done, but it's not easy. They haven't been connected
>
> 8 the phone yet so no one can ring. I think you have said in your letter
>
> 9 that you have been here once before, but I can't remember for sure. I know
>
> 10 you have ever wanted to travel around this part of England so why not
>
> 11 come and stay with me? The spare room, which I have just being finished
>
> 12 painting, has a wonderful view of the sea. I still have to arrange all the
>
> 13 furniture yet but if you've got some free time, then why not come and help
>
> 14 with this little job? I've been dying to show a friend around ever since
>
> 15 I got here so I'd love to see you if you haven't had made plans for
>
> your holiday.

b The correct lines in the text above also contain one word which *could* be removed without significantly changing the meaning of the text. Look back at the correct lines and see if you can identify the word in each case.

Example: (line 0) *last*

Unit 8 Relative clauses

> *Language focus:* defining and non-defining relative clauses; use of **whose, whom, where, when,** etc.; use of prepositions with relative clauses
>
> *Exam focus:*   open cloze question

LEAD-IN

1 The extracts below are from *The Guinness Book of Records*, which contains information on all world records. Before reading them, discuss with another student what the records under the following headings might be about.

WORKING CAREER   BEARD OF BEES   STANDING   HUMAN COMPUTER

Now read the passages below to see if you were right.

1 *LONGEST ON A RAFT*

The longest recorded survival alone on a raft is 133 days by Second Steward Poon Lim of the UK Merchant Navy, *whose ship was torpedoed in the Atlantic in 1942*.

2 *WORKING CAREER*

The longest working life has been that of 98 years by Mr Izumi, *who began work herding animals at a sugar mill at Isen, Tokunashima, Japan in 1872*. He retired as a sugar cane farmer in 1970 aged 105.

3 *MOST TRAVELLED MAN*

The man *who had visited more countries than anyone* was Jesse Hart Rosdail (1914–77). Of all the separately administered countries and territories listed in the *UN Population Report*, he had visited all, excepting only North Korea and the French Antarctic Territories.

4 *BEARD OF BEES*

The ultimate beard of bees was achieved by Max Beck, 21, of Arcola, USA, *who, in 1985, managed to attract 70,000 bees, weighing 9kg, to his body*.

5 *STANDING*

The longest period on record *that anyone has continuously stood* is for more than seventeen years in the case of Swami Maujgiri Maharij when performing the *Tapasya* or penance from 1955 to November 1973 in Shahjahanpur, India. When sleeping he would lean against a plank. He died aged 85 in 1980.

6 *HUMAN COMPUTER*

Mrs Shakuntala Devi of India demonstrated the multiplication of two 13-digit numbers, 7,686,369,774,870 × 2,465,099,745,779, *which were picked at random by the Computer Department of Imperial College London in June 1980*, in 28 seconds.

(adapted from *The Guinness Book of Records 1987 and 1994* © Guinness Publishing Ltd 1986 and 1993)

2 The grammatical term for the parts of the texts in italics is *relative clauses*. The two types of relative clause are described below.

a Defining relative clauses tell us exactly which person or thing the writer is talking about. Removing a defining relative clause completely changes the meaning of a sentence.

Example: *The man **who holds the record for golf-ball balancing** is Lang Martin. He balanced seven golf balls vertically without adhesive in 1980.*

b Non-defining relative clauses give us extra information about the person or thing the writer is talking about. Removing a non-defining clause does not significantly change the meaning of a sentence.

Example: *The oldest recorded bridegroom is Harry Stevens, 103, **who married 84-year-old Thelma Lucas at the Caravilla Retirement Home in Wisconsin.***

Look back at the extracts in Task 1 and decide whether the relative clauses they contain are (a) defining or (b) non-defining. Check your answers with another student.

3 Look at the extracts again and see if you can work out the rule for the use of commas with defining and non-defining relative clauses.

REFERENCE

1 In what type of relative clause are the following true? Read Sections A and B to find out and complete the chart with √s and Xs.

	Defining	*Non-defining*
Commas are used to separate the relative clause from the rest of the sentence		
The relative pronoun can be omitted		
That can be used instead of **who** or **which**		
When can be used as a relative pronoun		

A *Defining relative clauses*

1 Defining relative clauses help us identify or define the thing we are talking about.

A: *Do you know that man?*
B: *What man?*
A: *The man **who is talking to Mr Jones.***

We do not use commas before or after defining relative clauses.

2 **Who** is typically used for people; **which** or **that** are used to talk about things. **That** is also used for people in informal speech.

*Anyone **who** hasn't received a letter by now probably won't be called for interview. Even the train **that** left at 7 a.m. wouldn't have got us to London in time.*

3 **Who, that** and **which** are often left out when they are the object of a defining relative clause.

*I already know about the surprise (**which**) Peter has planned.* ('Peter' is the subject of the clause; 'which' is the object.)

But when **who, that** and **which** are the subject of a defining relative clause they cannot be left out.

*People **who** arrived late had to stand at the back.* (**not:** *People arrived late had to stand at the back.*)

4 Other relative pronouns in defining relative clauses are as follows:

*The woman **whose** house we're going to be staying in is quite a famous writer.* (possessive relative pronoun)
*Spring is the season **when** it's best to visit.* (used after nouns of time)
*There isn't a town in the southern half of the country **where** people can feel safe.* (used after nouns of place)
*I can't think of any reason **why** they should be late.* (used after the noun *reason*)

B *Non-defining relative clauses*

1 Non-defining relative clauses give extra information about a person or thing that we have already clearly identified in the sentence.

*The owner of the hotel, **who** had been at school with my mother, recognised her as soon as we walked in.*

A non-defining relative clause is separated from the rest of the sentence by commas.

2 In non-defining clauses **who** is used for people and **which** (not **that**) is used for things.

*I've received your letter, **which** I've passed on to my boss.*

3 We also use **which** in non-defining relative clauses when we want to talk about the whole previous clause.

*She's decided to go to college, **which** has really pleased her parents.*

4 In non-defining clauses we can never omit the relative pronoun.

*The key is in my wallet, **which** I've left at home.*

5 Other relative pronouns and non-defining clauses are as follows:

*Margaret Spool, **whose** children's stories have won her international fame, has just produced her first novel.*
*Shall I call back later, **when** you're not quite so busy?* (used after expressions of time)
*I'll give you my friend's home number, **where** I can be reached most evenings.* (used after expressions of place)

2 Read the pairs of sentences below and match each sentence to one of the explanations (i) and (ii) that follow.

1 a) I chose the cat that still had its tail.
   b) I chose the cat, which still had its tail.

   i) I chose the cat, probably from a group of different animals. It still had its tail (perhaps some of the others didn't).
   ii) From a group of cats I chose the one with a tail.

2 a) I found the letter which she had been writing earlier in the sitting room.
   b) I found the letter, which she had been writing earlier, in the sitting room.

   i) She was writing the letter in the sitting room.
   ii) I found the letter in the sitting room.

3 a) He was wearing some sunglasses, which I liked.
   b) He was wearing some sunglasses that I liked.

   i) I liked the fact that he was wearing sunglasses.
   ii) I liked the sunglasses he was wearing.

4 a) To cheer her up I gave her a clock which worked.
   b) To cheer her up I gave her a clock, which worked.

   i) I gave her a clock and my action cheered her up.
   ii) I gave her a clock which worked, as opposed to one that didn't.

C *Prepositions with relative clauses*

1 In defining and non-defining relative clauses in conversation we usually place a dependent preposition at the end of the clause:

*The people (who) I was speaking **to** didn't seem interested.*
*I met Kevin, **who** I got the job **through**, quite by chance.*

In formal written English we often put the preposition before **whom** or **which**:

*That's the person **to** whom David was introduced.*

After a preposition we cannot use **who** and **that**; we can only use **whom** and **which**.

2 Note the special phrases in non-defining clauses:

some all both many much	of which	whom

*I made a lot of good friends at evening classes, **many of whom** I still see.*

3 Complete the sentences below with one of the relative clauses a–h and add any necessary punctuation. Then check your answers with another student.

1 It's important to find a house ....

2 The person .... is a good friend of mine.

3 My son's been to places ....

4 There is not going to be a strike ....

5 The director of the school .... used to work in Spain.

6 We're having a reunion of some old school friends ....

7 That old car over there ....
is worth a lot of money.

8 I know a great resort ....

a) that I've never heard of
b) which has good amenities nearby
c) which I haven't used for years
d) most of whom you'll recognise
e) you'll be meeting
f) which is a great relief to everyone
g) where you have the beaches to yourself
h) whose name I forget

COMMUNICATIVE PRACTICE

1 The case of Samuel Ruddock

Read about the mysterious events that happened to Samuel Ruddock. Discuss with another student what seems strange about the story. The numbers and spaces in the text mark places where you could put the non-defining relative clauses a–k listed below. Solve the mystery and find the motive(s) for the crime by inserting the clauses in the text. The first one has been done for you.

Samuel Ruddock had been living alone in his large house since the departure of his children and wife (1) ...*a*... . Samuel (2) .... went to bed on 6th November 1937 with his evening cup of tea (3) .... He made his way upstairs and, after checking that the windows were tightly secured, he locked the bedroom door and settled down into his large four-poster bed (4) .... The clock on the wall (5) .... had just chimed the first stroke of midnight as he fell into a deep sleep.

He awoke to the sound of three large policemen breaking down his bedroom door: they had been called after neighbours had heard a woman screaming. The clock (6) .... said it was one minute after midnight. Samuel found himself lying on the floor, next to the body of his estranged wife (7) .... She had been shot. The gun (8) .... was lying between them. The room (9) .... was completely empty except for the clock on the wall.

No one from the Police Department of Arkansas State (10) .... believed his story about going to bed at midnight. He was charged with the murder of his wife Jean (11) ....

a) which he had caused by his insensitivity to his wife's illness
b) which had been put forward an hour
c) from which everything (including the bed) had been removed
d) who had since written his children out of his will
e) which was just as she had planned
f) under which someone was hiding
g) which had now been put back an hour
h) which had a law making invalid any will written by someone insane
i) which he had at some time held
j) which had been drugged
k) whose doctor had predicted she had only three months to live

2 Collage connections

Look at the collage of pictures and images below and with another student try and identify two or three people or things between whom/which there is a connection.

Example: *Three symbols that represent different foreign currencies.*

Find as many connections as you can and write them down in the form of problems for other students to solve, using a relative clause.

Example: *Find three symbols that represent different foreign currencies.*

EXAM FOCUS

EXAM TIP 10

Punctuation

Looking at the punctuation of sentences in the open cloze task in Part 2 can help you to work out the missing words. With relative clauses, for example, a comma before the blank which stands for a relative pronoun indicates a non-defining relative clause, so you would use **which**, not **that**, to talk about things.

HURRY UP AND GET TO THE POINT

In the following passages all the blanks are words which relate to the grammar of relative clauses covered in this unit.

1 Open cloze

The text below is adapted from the Introduction to the novel *The Day of the Triffids*. Read the text and think of the word which best fits each space. Use only *one* word in each space.

John Wyndham, (1) .... was born in 1903, lived in Edgbaston, Birmingham, until 1911 and then in many other parts of England. After attending several English preparatory schools he went to Bedales School from 1918 till 1921. Careers (2) .... he tried included farming, law, commercial art and advertising, and he first started writing short stories (3) .... were intended for sale in 1925. From 1930 till 1939 he wrote stories of different kinds for American publications but the names under (4) .... he wrote varied. During the war he was in the Civil Service and afterwards in the Army. In 1946 he went back to writing short stories, (5) .... which he had some success in the USA, and he decided to try a modified form of what is unhappily known as 'science fiction'. He wrote *The Day of the Triffids* and *The Kraken Wakes*, ((6) .... of which have been translated into several languages), *The Chrysalids* and *The Midwich Cuckoos*, (7) .... was made into a film entitled *The Village of the Damned*. He wrote many other fine novels, (8) .... titles include *The Seeds of Time, Trouble with Lichen* and *The Outward Urge*, all (9) .... which have been published by Penguin Books. John Wyndham died in March 1969, at a time (10) .... man was about to take his first steps on the moon.

(adapted from the Introduction to *The Day of the Triffids*, Penguin 1987)

Unit 9 **Verb and object patterns**

> *Language focus:* transitive and intransitive verbs; verbs with direct and indirect objects; use of **to** and **for** with indirect objects
>
> *Exam focus:* multiple-choice cloze and error correction questions

LEAD-IN

Not all verbs in English can be used with objects. For example, you can't 'disappear something' – you have to say 'something disappears'.

Verbs that *can* be used with objects (e.g. **hit** something) do not all follow the same object pattern. For example:

The car hit a tree. (verb + direct object)
He gave me a book. (verb + indirect and direct objects)

1 Working with another student, fit the jigsaw pieces below into the jigsaw board. For a piece to fit it must be both the right shape and fit grammatically with the verb. One line has been done for you.

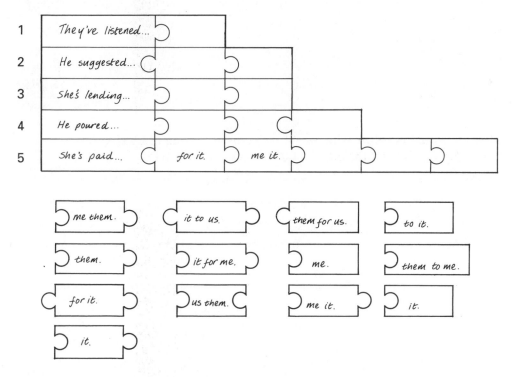

2 Look back at line 5 in the puzzle. Working with another student, try and work out what kind of noun *it* could stand for in each case.

REFERENCE

A Transitive and intransitive verbs

1 *Transitive* verbs are those which are followed by an object:
*Someone in the crowd **threw a stone** which **hit the policeman**.*

They can be used in the passive form:
*The pupils **were welcomed** by the school principal.*

2 *Intransitive* verbs are those which cannot be used with an object:
*My passport **has disappeared**.*
*No one **has arrived** yet.*

Verbs which are typically used intransitively are:

appear	arrive	consist	decline	depart	die	disappear	drip
fall	flow	grow	happen	itch	lie	listen	recur	rise
succeed (meaning 'have success')		vibrate	wait				

We can thus *not* say: *he succeeded the test*, or *the rain grew the flowers* or *they listened the children to the music*.

To express such meanings we need to use an alternative transitive verb – *He **passed** the test* – or a structure with **make** or **let**:
*The rain **made** the flowers grow.*
*They **let** the children listen to the music.*

NOTE: Intransitive verbs cannot be used in the passive form. We cannot say: *The plan was succeeded.*

1 Complete the sentences below with one of the verbs at the end of each sentence. One of the verbs is intransitive and the other is typically used transitively.

1 Unemployment .... to record levels last month.   (raise / rise)

2 Many children had to leave the cities during the war and were .... by strangers.   (bring up / grow up)

3 He grabbed the parcel from the postman and .... it to see what was inside.   (shake / vibrate)

4 The car skidded on the ice and .... a litter bin at the side of the road. (knock over / fell over)

5 If signs of the illness .... , contact your local doctor immediately. (recur / repeat)

6 You'll never .... your ambitions if you don't work harder. (achieve / succeed)

7 Several guests have .... the hotel this morning and taken their keys with them.   (depart / leave)

8 Has anyone .... anything to you about getting our money back for the trip we missed?   (say / speak)

9 The number of students enrolling in courses at the language school is .... (reduce / decline)

10 I accidentally knocked my cup over and .... coffee on the new carpet. (spill / drip)

B *Transitive verbs and object patterns*

1 Many common verbs have two objects: a direct object and an indirect object.
   *The waiter **showed** me the menu.*

   (**me** is the indirect object, **the menu** is the direct object)

2 The indirect object can also be introduced by the prepositions **to** or **for**. In this case, it comes *after* the direct object:
   *She didn't want to tell the bad news **to the children**.*

   (compare: *She didn't want to tell the children the bad news.*)

   The preposition is usually used when the indirect object is a longer phrase.
   *My mother **has lent** our spare television **to the elderly man next door**.*
   *The child **saved** a seat **for the friend she was expecting**.*

   Verbs typically used in this way with **to** are:

give	lend	pass	promise	read
rent	send	show	tell	write

   Verbs typically used in this way with **for** are:

book	buy	draw	leave	make	pour
prepare	reserve	save	steal	take

3 Verb + direct object + **to** + indirect object

   There is a certain group of verbs in English with which we *have to* use **to** before an indirect object.
   *He **explained** the scheme **to the foreign visitors**.*
   We cannot say: *He explained the foreign visitors the scheme.*

   Verbs which follow this pattern are:

address	admit	describe	explain	introduce
mention	propose	recommend	suggest	

2 Complete the sentences below with the two 'objects' given in brackets at the end of each sentence. Think about in which *order* they should be used and whether you need to *add a preposition or not.*

Example: *The man in the market **sold** me a broken watch.*　　　(a broken watch / me)

1 That's the estate agent that **got** ....

(the house / my parents)

2 She hasn't managed to **prove** ....

(anyone / her innocence)

3 When was the last time the headmaster **ordered** .... ?

(the school / any new equipment)

4 The happy father rushed out to **announce** ....

(the rest of the family / the news)

5 The college **has offered** ....

(my sister / a place on the course)

6 The company **owes** ....

(a foreign bank / a large sum of money)

7 Some people I knew from work **found** ....

(the flat / us)

8 I'd like you to **teach** ....

(French / all the classes in the school)

Find the two verbs in this exercise which follow the pattern of the verbs in Section B (3).

COMMUNICATIVE PRACTICE

1 Fairytales

First tell another student what you know about these fairytales.

a) Cinderella　　　b) Little Red Riding Hood　　　c) The Three Bears
d) Snow White and the Seven Dwarfs　　　e) Jack and the Beanstalk

Now, working with another student, complete sentences 1–8 on the opposite page to make a true statement about an event in one of the fairytales. To do this use two of the words (direct / indirect objects) from the box below. You may need to add a preposition. Then put in the brackets at the end of each sentence a letter to show which fairytale you are talking about.

Example: *A woman gave her son a cow. (e)*

her son	their sister	one of her hosts	dinner	his mother
some food	her	her grandmother	herself	a golden hen
someone else's name	a shoe	nothing to eat	a prince	seven men
her grandmother's hands	her	a cow		

1 A little girl decided to go through the forest to take .... (.....)

2 Two women laughed when someone offered .... (.....)

3 A queen got angry when her mirror suggested .... (.....)

4 A poor boy stole .... (.....)

5 A little girl with golden hair left .... (.....)

6 A girl didn't introduce .... (.....)

7 A lovely woman regularly prepared .... (.....)

8 A loving child described .... (.....)

2 Noughts and crosses

The game on the board below is played in a similar way to a normal game of noughts and crosses. One player is 'noughts' and the other 'crosses'. The object of the game is to get a row of three XXX or three OOO.

Play with another student. Using one of the grids on the board, choose a square and make an offer to your partner about the picture or words in the square, using one of the verbs on the board. You must use the words *you / your / to you / for you*. No verb can be used twice in any one game.

Example: *Grid 1: I can recommend a hotel to you.*

If your partner thinks that your offer makes sense, and is grammatically correct, you can put your nought or cross on the square. If not, he / she must explain why. If you can't agree, ask your teacher to act as judge.

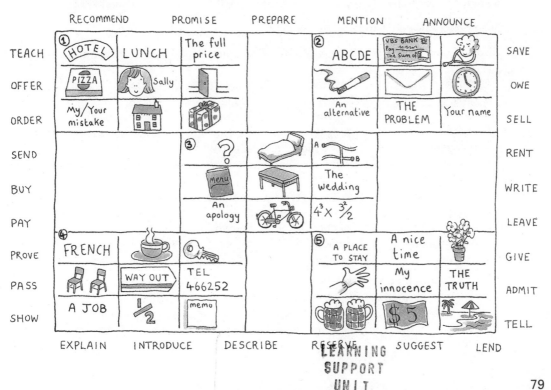

EXAM FOCUS

1 Multiple-choice cloze

Read the text below and decide which answer A, B, C or D best fits each space.

A strange history

Mexican General Antonio Lopez de Santa Anna (1814–76) was somewhat accident-prone. Throughout the 1830s the Mexicans were (1) .... in a number of battles with the Texans. On 20 April 1836, Santa Anna (2) .... up camp at the San Jacinto River, overlooking a wood where the Texans were (3) .... to be hiding. Given the circumstances it was perhaps a little unwise to (4) .... his troops to take a siesta, for in the middle of their afternoon nap the entire Mexican army was overpowered by the Texans in just eighteen minutes. Santa Anna (5) .... to escape on horseback but was not as fortunate when, fighting the French in December 1838, he lost a leg. For the next four years, Santa Anna (6) .... the leg at his hacienda near Vercruz until, on 26 September 1842, by which time he had virtually (7) .... dictator of Mexico, he arranged a special burial service (8) .... the detached limb. To the accompaniment of bands and orchestras, his supporters solemnly paraded the leg through the streets of Mexico city before (9) .... it to rest in a national shrine (10) .... as the Pantheon of Saint Paula. Two years later the leg was (11) .... during riots that marked Santa Anna's fall from power and (12) .... without trace.

(adapted from *The Guinness Book of Oddities* © Guinness Publishing Ltd and Geoff Tibballs 1995)

1	A	fought	B	involved	C	appeared	D fallen
2	A	grew	B	brought	C	made	D set
3	A	used	B	known	C	spoken	D managed
4	A	order	B	suggest	C	explain	D propose
5	A	managed	B	succeeded	C	achieved	D arrived
6	A	remained	B	reserved	C	stayed	D kept
7	A	risen	B	grown	C	become	D made
8	A	about	B	to	C	because	D for
9	A	laying	B	laid	C	lied	D lying
10	A	called	B	named	C	known	D believed
11	A	disappeared	B	robbed	C	stolen	D departed
12	A	missed	B	went	C	disappeared	D displaced

EXAM TIP 11

Collecting mistakes

The error correction exercise in Part 4 is based on errors that students commonly make when writing in English. A good way to prepare yourself for this task is to keep a record of all the one-word-too-many mistakes that you and perhaps other students in your class make in your writing throughout your FCE course.

2 Error correction

a   Before doing the exam type exercise in part b discuss with another student the one-word-too-many mistakes that students have made in the sentences below. All the language points relate to the 'object pattern' grammar in this unit.

1   He picked up the bag and then disappeared it.
2   She said me that she had had fun.
3   Please let me introduce you my friend John.
4   Prices were rose sharply last year.
5   They saved for my friend a seat.
6   The teacher explained us the point.

b   Read the text below and look carefully at each line. Some of the lines are correct and some have a word which should not be there. If a line is correct, put a tick by it. If a line has a word which should not be there, write the word at the end of the line. There are two examples at the beginning (0 and 00).

Meeting old friends

0   I went out with an old school friend a few months ago. We hadn't   ✓

00   seen each other for ages but I had heard she was working nearby me so   *me*

1   I phoned her. We had a lot to catch up on. We told to each other about

2   everything that had happened since we last met and discussed about how

3   life was different in the world of work from our school days. Although I

4   enjoyed seeing with my friend again, it made me feel sad that all the fun of

5   my youth now seemed to belong to the past. I suggested her that we meet the

6   following week and that we try and get a few more of the old gang to come

7   along. She agreed. I paid for the bill and watched her leave wondering

8   whether we really would meet up with our old friends again. Well, the

9   following week four of us met. Two weeks later there were six and now

10   the number has reached to ten. It seems that we all missed the old times

11   and regretted not keeping in touch. Making the effort to see old friends isn't

12   easy but we were succeeded and in just a few months so much has changed.

13   Tim has offered us his holiday home in Spain, Janice has found a new

14   job through Sarah and I've found for Karen a new bedsit. We've all enjoyed

15   feeling young again, which I, like everyone else, was looking for it.

Unit 10 Comparatives and superlatives

Language focus: comparative and superlative forms of adjectives and adverbs; **(not) as
... as;** words and expressions that can be used before comparatives

Exam focus: key-word transformation and open cloze questions

LEAD-IN

1 Read through the text and decide whether the highlighted words are (a) comparative
adjective forms, or (b) comparative adverb forms. Check your answers with another
student.

Improve your memory

Did you know that everything you have ever
read or seen is stored somewhere in your
memory? The problem is that you can't
always get at it. And when you can't get at
something in your memory, you say you
have a poor memory. In fact, you don't have
a poor memory at all – you have a wonderful
memory. But to use that memory (1) **more
effectively** it has to be trained.

That's why memory training is such an
important part of the unique Pelman Home
Study Course. As a Pelman student, your
personal tutor will guide you through a
series of lessons which become progressively
(2) **more difficult** – each one based on
programmed learning techniques that will
train your memory to achieve a (3) **higher**
level of performance.

INSTANT RECALL

This is possible because your memory is like
a muscle. Without exercise it gets flabby.
But with the right kind of training, you'll be
able to recall things much (4) **faster**.

Right from the start you will feel your
memory muscles getting (5) **stronger** – your
powers of recall ever (6) **quicker**.

Many people just do not realise how much
they can improve their memories and the
extent to which it can make them (7) **more
successful** in their business and social lives.
There is simply no one who cannot learn to
retain things (8) **longer** and recall things
(9) **more quickly**. A trained memory can
truly be a passport to a (10) **better** life!

WHO CAN BENEFIT?
• Students   • Industrial workers
• Salespeople   • Professional people
• Managers   – In fact, anyone!
• Office workers

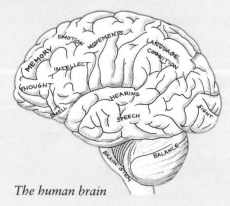

The human brain

(adapted from a Pelman advertisement)

2 Below are two incomplete grammar rules about: (a) how to form comparative adjectives, and (b) how to form comparative adverbs.

By looking at the evidence from the Improve your memory advertisement, complete each rule using the language in the box below. Work with another student to do this.

> add -er   more   e.g. **quickly**   more   **longer**   one syllable
> e.g. **fast runner/run fast**   -er ending

a To form the comparative form of adjectives with (1) ....

e.g. **quick**, (2) .... With words of more than one

syllable, e.g. **successful**, use (3) .... in front of the word.

b To form the comparative form of adverbs use (1) ....

in front of those adverbs which have an **-ly** ending (2) ....

Adjectives, however, which have the same adverb form (3) ....

.... also have the same (4) ....

in the adverb form, e.g. (5) ....

REFERENCE

1 Use this exercise to see how much you already know about the comparative forms of adjectives and adverbs. Complete each sentence below with one of the words or phrases which follow it. Discuss your answers with another student and then check your answers by looking at Sections A–E below.

1 The USA is probably the world's .... country.   (richer / richest)

2 Can we go somewhere .... to talk?   (quieter / more quiet)

3 I can't remember a spring that was .... than this.   (hoter / hotter)

4 I really think she talks even .... than she used to.
(quicker / more quickly)

5 The meal was all right, but it was .... the film.
(less good than / not as good as)

6 The costumes and lighting were terrible and the acting was .... as bad.
(even / just)

7 Of all the countries I've been to, France is the one of which I have .... the
fondest memories.   (by far / far)

8 Chinese is the most widely spoken language .... the world.   (in / of)

A *Adjectives: Comparative and superlative forms*

Adjective	Comparative form	Superlative form
Adjectives of one syllable: high fast warm cheap	**-er** higher faster warmer cheaper	**the -est** the highest the fastest
Adjectives of more than one syllable: expensive difficult helpful	**more . . . less** more expensive more difficult less helpful	**the most . . . the least** the most expensive the most difficult the least helpful
Irregular forms: good bad far	good – better bad – worse far – further	good – the best bad – the worst far – the furthest

*Life just seems to be getting **more expensive** each week.*
*Taking the train proved to be **the cheapest** option.*
*Christmas is one of **the warmest** times of the year in Australia.*

NOTE: Some comparative forms involve a change of spelling:
big – bigger   hot – hotter   fat – fatter   happy – happier   easy – easier

And a few two-syllable words also have the **-er/-est** comparative/superlative form:
quieter, narrower, simpler.

B *Adverbs: Comparative and superlative forms*

Adverb	Comparative form	Superlative form
Adverbs with -ly ending carefully clearly	**more** carefully **less** clearly	**the most** carefully **the least** clearly
Adverbs with same *form as adjective:* fast hard high	**-er** faster harder	**the -est** the fastest the hardest

*Do your homework **more carefully** and you'll get better marks.*
*I work **harder** than anyone but no one seems to notice.*
*I was surprised that of all the speakers the Prime Minister spoke **the least clearly**.*

C *as . . . as*

When comparing things we can also use adjectives and adverbs with (**not**) **as . . . as**.
*The car looks **as new as** when we bought it.*
*Your son is behaving just **as aggressively as** before.*
*That clock isn't **as reliable as** the one in the kitchen.*

Not as . . . (as) is used instead of **less** with one-syllable adjectives / adverbs that usually have an **-er** comparative form.

*My father hasn't been working **as hard as** he used to.* (not: *less hard.*)
*The exam wasn't **as easy as** the last one.* (not: *less easy than.*)

D *Words and expressions used before comparatives*

even	a lot	much	far	a bit	any	. . . (lazier / more helpful)

just	every bit	not nearly	nowhere near	. . . (as lazy as)

*This car is **even slower** than the last one we had.*
*Have we got **much further** to go?*
*The team were **nowhere near as good** in defence this year.*
*The countryside must suit you: you seem **a lot more relaxed**.*

The phrase **by far** can also be used with superlatives in a similar way.

*Come on, don't be modest. I've heard you were **by far the best** student **in** the class.*

Also note this use of the preposition **in** after superlatives.

2 Work with another student and match the half sentences on the left to those on the right to form complete sentences.

1 The journey by train was less
2 The seats on trains are nowhere near as
3 We can deliver parcels even more
4 I found the exam
5 With the right tool we finished it
6 The team did not perform as
7 We must have walked
8 Of all the performances, his was the
9 The whole event went far
10 The people we met there were the

a) easier this time round.
b) more smoothly this time.
c) further than I thought.
d) enjoyable than before.
e) well as it could have.
f) nice these days.
g) much more easily.
h) most hospitable of all.
i) least convincing.
j) quickly than before.

COMMUNICATIVE PRACTICE

1 Superlative impostor

Look at the lists of four things / people / places below. In each list, there are three true superlatives; that is, the biggest, highest, most valuable, etc. One thing in each list is an impostor: that is, it may only be the second or third biggest, best, etc. With two or three other students, look at each list and discuss which one the impostor might be.

1 SIZE: Lake Michigan   the Pacific Ocean   the River Nile   the Caspian Sea

2 AREA: Canada   Asia   Russia   Greenland

3 MONEY: USA   the Sultan of Brunei   Van Gogh   gold

4 NUMBER OF PEOPLE: Mexico City   China   English   Chinese

5 SIZE: Mount Everest   the Empire State Building   Jupiter   the Sahara

6 WEATHER CONDITIONS: Ethiopia   Antarctica   the North Pole   Bangladesh

7 ANIMALS: leopard   ostrich   great white shark   giraffe

2 Where on earth am I?

Look at the map of the world and identify a country that you know reasonably well and can answer simple questions on, such as on climate and population.

The other members of the class have to find out which country you have chosen. They can ask you ten questions, all of which have to be in the form of comparatives.

Example questions:

Is the country further north than (Egypt)?
Does the country have a warmer climate than (Britain)?
Does it have borders with more than one other country?
Is it as industrialised as (Western European countries)?
Is the capital of the country larger than (Paris)?
Which is closer to the country: (Japan) or (Norway)?

Example answers:

Yes, much . . . -er.   No, *not at all.*
Yes, a bit more.   No, *nowhere near.*
Yes, quite a lot more.   No, *not as . . . as.*
                      No, *much less . . . .*

Before you start, prepare a few questions which you might ask to identify the general part of the world a country is in and two or three questions which might help you to identify a country more specifically.

EXAM FOCUS

EXAM TIP 12

The key to the change

There are two steps that you should follow in
completing the key-word transformation task
in Part 3. First, use the key-word to identify
the structure which the question is testing.
Then, think carefully about all the changes to
the first sentence which will be necessary.

1 Key-word transformation

Complete the second sentence so that it has a similar meaning to the first sentence, using
the key-word given. Do not change the key-word. You must use between two and five
words, including the key-word.

Example: *It's not as difficult as before.*
It's <u>less difficult than</u> before.   **less**

1 I didn't realise we had wandered such a long way from the path.

   We had wandered .... the path than I realised.   **much**

2 My friend has always been able to cook better than me.

   I have never been able to cook .... my friend.   **as**

3 Going by train is much faster than going by car.

   Going by car .... going by train.   **takes**

4 I'm afraid I don't have a cheaper one in stock.

   I'm afraid this .... I have in stock.   **the**

5 Michael Jackson is the performer I would most like to meet.

   I'd like to meet Michael Jackson .... performer.   **other**

6 We had to pay more for the tickets than I expected.

   The tickets were .... I expected.   **not**

7 We had the same number of players injured as the other team.

   We had .... players injured as the other team.   **many**

8 The test was much easier than I thought it would be.

   The test was .... I thought it would be.   **nowhere**

9 I hated the resort and liked the hotel even less.

   I thought the hotel .... the resort.   **worse**

10 They were asking higher prices than usual for front row tickets.

   They weren't selling front row tickets .... usual.   **as**

EXAM TIP 13

Looking beyond your nose

In the open cloze task in Part 2, you must find words which fit *grammatically* in each space. However, you must also think about how the words you choose fit in the *context* of the passage. To do this you may well need to read beyond the immediate sentence. For example, look at how the words you need in the first sentence below are indicated by information in the second and third sentences of the passage.

2 Open cloze

The following text is about the USA's vast open state of Wyoming and the important part this state has played in American history.

Read the text and, working with another student, think carefully about whether a comparative or a superlative structure is related to the missing word. Then complete the text, using only *one* word in each space.

Wyoming

Wyoming is the USA's (1) .... populated state. No other state has (2) ....

people – only 465,000. There are no big cities. The (3) .... city of the few that there

are is the capital Cheyenne, home to 50,000 people. Yet the state is rich in mineral deposits,

natural beauty and history. Coal lies under 55 per cent of Wyoming and in the Powder River

Basin towering coal silos announce from a distance that you are approaching the largest coal

mine (4) .... the Americas, Black Thunder. Indeed, it was here in the wilderness that

I saw (5) .... far the biggest dump truck that I had (6) .... seen.

   Historically, South Pass – the old Oregon wagon trail – is Wyoming's (7) ....

significant landmark. South Pass offered the (8) .... , though not the most direct,

wagon route for settlers over the Rocky Mountains, and had it not been for South Pass, the

USA might be (9) .... smaller today. South Pass City, born in a gold boom, played

another key role in US history. Its governing body, the Wyoming Territorial Legislature, proved

itself to be (10) .... most progressive in the world when it became the first

governing body to extend full voting rights to women.

(adapted from Thomas J. Abercrombie, 'Wide Open Wyoming', *National Geographic*)

Unit 11 The future

Language focus: uses of **will** / **going to** / present continuous / present simple to talk about the future; uses of future perfect and future continuous tenses

Exam focus: open cloze and error correction questions

LEAD-IN

1 Complete your 'futurescope' below with information about yourself. Make notes in each of the boxes.

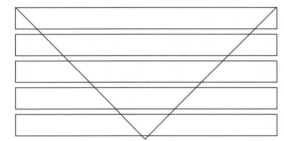

Arrangements for later today

A resolution for the rest of the year

Holiday plans

You and FCE: a prediction

Career / job in ten years' time

2 Now look at this short text about a famous British actor and match the highlighted verb phrases to the future meanings a–e.

a) talking about intentions
b) talking about arrangements
c) making predictions
d) talking about a future action in progress at a particular time
e) talking about timetables / schedules

Blessed to attempt an Everest record

Actor Brian Blessed aims to push back the frontier of middle age by being the oldest man to climb Mount Everest.

"It's not how old you are, it's how you're old," said Blessed, who climbed to 26,000 feet in his first attempt on Everest three years ago.

His obsession with Everest goes back to his childhood hero George Mallory, who disappeared near the summit in 1924. It was Mallory who, when asked why he wanted to climb Everest, gave the celebrated reply: "Because it is there."

Blessed said: (1) "We**'ll** probably never **know** if Mallory made it to the summit, and I wholly embrace the mystery."

The attempt (2) **begins** next Tuesday

"IT'S NOT HOW OLD YOU ARE, IT'S HOW YOU'RE OLD."

when the group set off for base camp . As part of his mission Blessed (3) **is going to place** on top of Everest a white scarf given to him by the Dalai Lama. "He's asked me to recite a mantra and a peace prayer for the world."

Blessed (4) **is** also **taking** with him a teddy bear which is to be auctioned later to raise money for children suffering from cancer.

Blessed says he wants to spend the rest of his life devoting six months a year to acting and the other six to adventure. This time next year (5) **he'll be setting off** in search of the Abominable Snowman. "I want to climb the highest summit on each of the seven continents, plug the ozone hole, explore the bottom of the sea," he said.

(adapted from the *Evening Standard*)

3 Look back at your 'futurescope' and make your notes into full sentences. Think carefully about the verb form in each case.

Example: *I'm collecting my photos this afternoon.*

Now ask your partner questions to find out about the information in his / her futurescope. Think carefully about the verb form you use in your questions.

Example:

A: *What are you doing later today?*
B: *I'm going home for dinner first, then meeting some friends.*

REFERENCE

Main forms used to express future meaning

1 Will

Affirmative   *Negative*
I will (I'll, etc.) come, etc.   I will not (won't) come, etc.

Question   *Short answers*
Will you come?   Yes, I will. No, I won't.

2 Be going to

Affirmative   *Negative*
I am (I'm) going to come, etc.   I am not (I'm not) going to come, etc.

Question   *Short answers*
Are you going to come?   Yes, I am. No, I'm not.

3 Present continuous

I am coming, etc.

Uses

1 Will

a **Will** is used to make predictions based on a personal opinion or what the speaker believes to be the usual course of events.

We'll have time for a drink before the film starts.
The train won't get us there in time.

It is often used with this kind of meaning with the following verbs and phrases:

I think, I expect, I doubt, I suppose, I guess, I'm sure.

I doubt there will be anything to eat, just drinks.
The police will search fans as they enter the stadium, I suppose.

b The contracted form of **will** (**'ll**) is used when the speaker decides something at the moment of speaking.

'Please come, Ruth, everyone's expecting you.'
'OK, stop going on, I'll come.'

c **Will** is also used with the following kinds of meaning.

Requests and offers:

Will you help me do the garden later?
Don't worry, I'll help you with whatever needs doing.

Promises and threats:

I promise I'll be there on time.
We won't let you have your friends round if you don't tidy your room.

Refusals:

Our shop won't give you your money back without the receipt.
The matches won't light, they're too damp.

Also: machines and illnesses:

The fridge door won't shut.
My cold won't go away.

NOTE: **Shall** is not typically used instead of **will** in everyday English but is used in the interrogative form with I and **we** to ask for and make suggestions and to make offers.

Shall we go to the Italian restaurant for a change?
What shall I do if he's not in?
I'll make you a cup of tea, shall I?

d In sentences involving link words and phrases such as **when, before, after, as soon as, in case** and **until** we usually only use **will** *once* in the sentence.

I'll give you a ring as soon as I've heard from her.
I'll give you the phone number in case you get lost.

1 Complete the sentences below. Use contracted forms if you want to.

1 I really .... expect that they .... turn up this late.

2 .... I call back later if you're busy?

3 You'll probably be too tired to come, I .... ?

4 I'm phoning to tell you I .... be late. The car .... start.

5 We're stuck here until Philip arrives, so what .... we do while we're waiting?

6 I .... phone Sarah in case she .... know we're coming.

7 I .... return the book to you as soon as I .... read it.

8 I .... if she .... recognise you. You've really changed.

LEARNING
SUPPORT
UNIT

2 Be going to

a **Be going to** is used when someone has a definite intention or plan to do something. It can express determination to do something.

*The council **is going to** knock down the old cinema to make a new shopping centre.*
*I'm **going to** go tonight whether you like it or not.*

b **Be going to** is used to make or ask for predictions in response to something which exists in the present situation.

*Look, that child **is going to** fall if she's not careful!*
*Who **is going to** clean up this mess?*

3 Present continuous

The present continuous tense is used to talk about definite arrangements / fixed plans in the future, such as ones that appear in appointment books and calendar programmes.

*We're **not having** the barbeque on Sunday now, I'm afraid.*
*The BBC **are showing** Sunday's match live in twenty-six countries.*

It is used with a definite future time reference, whether stated (as a time phrase) or understood.

2 **Complete the sentences by putting the verb at the end of each sentence into the correct form to express future meaning.**

1 I'll have to prepare the meal before we .... out.   (go)

2 I've got a terrible headache which .... away.   (not / go)

3 .... we .... at your place, say about sixish?   (meet)

4 I can't meet you on Friday, the plumber ....   (come)

5 OK, you've convinced me, we .... the train.   (take)

6 I .... this essay even if I have to stay up all night.   (finish)

7 .... anyone .... that phone? (not / answer)

8 Do you know how you .... to the party yet?   (get)

9 We .... the children while you go shopping.   (look after)

10 The town .... the annual spring festival on 5th May this year.   (hold)

4 Present simple

The present simple is used with future meaning when talking about timetables or programmes of events.

*The 100m race **starts** at two o'clock after the long-jump final.*
*The train **arrives** at platform four and **departs** at 4.15.*

NOTE: We use the present form of **to be** in the following phrases with future meaning:

*I would invite you in but **we're about to** go out.*
*Today's news means thousands **are likely to** lose their jobs.*
*Jack's **supposed to** come too but I don't think he will.*
*Don't worry about the exam, you're **bound to** pass.*

3 Match these examples to the different uses described in Boxes 5–6 below. Write the examples in the boxes.

1 I'll be calling in later, can I bring you anything?
2 By the time I retire I'll have worked here for twenty-three years.
3 We will have built the new stadium by next season.
4 I'm sure the restaurant will be making money before long.
5 I've got a letter for Henry. Will you be seeing him today?
6 I won't have finished the report before the meeting.
7 This time next week I'll be lying in the sun in Greece.
8 We'll have been married six years this April.

5 Future continuous

> I / you / he / she / it / we / they **will** + **be** + verb + **ing**
>
> **a** The future continuous tense is used to predict an action that will be in progress at some time in the future. Examples:
>
> ....
>
> ....
>
> **b** It is sometimes used when talking or asking about personal plans. This form sounds slightly more formal than the present continuous. Examples:
>
> ....
>
> ....

6 Future perfect

> I / you / he / she / it / we / they **will** + **have** + past participle
>
> **a** The future perfect tense is used to talk about an action or event which will, or will not, be complete at some specific point in the future. Examples:
>
> ....
>
> ....
>
> **b** It is used to talk about the length of time an action will have lasted at some point in the future. Examples:
>
> ....
>
> ....

4 Recording the use of a particular time phrase with a particular tense is a useful way of remembering how a tense is used. Look at the unfinished sentences and the future time phrases below. Write in the boxes phrases that could complete each sentence. Some words can be used with both sentences.

as you read this letter   until tomorrow   on time   by March
all day tomorrow   before then   for a few weeks   soon

1 I'll be working there . . .

2 I'll have finished it . . .

COMMUNICATIVE PRACTICE

1 That's not it

Get into groups of two or three and then write four or five cards as follows:

Think of a famous person (politician, sports person, film star, etc.) or someone in your school who is known to the rest of the class.

Take a strip of paper or card and on one side write his or her name *in large letters*. On the other side, write some true information about this person's *future*. It might be:

future arrangement   *future plan*   or   *future happening*

but *not a prediction*.

How to play

1 In turns, each group holds up a card so that the rest of the class can see the name.

2 The rest of the class then have to find out the information on the back of the card by asking questions like:

Isn't he going to produce a new album with . . . ?

The group with the card answers 'Yes' or 'No'.

3 The group who ask the correct question are given the card. The group with the most cards at the end of the game are the winners.

2 Stock exchange

Working with another student, imagine that you have £1,000 to invest in three of the stocks below. Which stocks are likely to go up or down in value? Read the newspaper headlines and think about how the news stories may affect the value of the stocks. (The prices given are the real prices of the stocks on the London Stock Exchange on 7th December 1993, and the headlines are from newspapers of the same day.)

When you have made your decisions, your teacher will tell you how each stock finished that day and you can work out how much you have gained or lost.

Company	Opening price	Your investment	Closing share price: up or down
ERA Toys	0.10		
Midlands Electricity	6.53		
Iceland Foods*	1.54		
British Petroleum	3.26		
British Airways	4.33		
Manchester United†	5.37		

*a chain of food shops
†a football team

Worst winter in years still to come

More Britons seeking Xmas in the sun

Weather keeps seasonal shoppers at home

Further fall in oil price

BP chief says cost-cutting plan is working

Iceland Foods still opposed to Sunday trading

MANCHESTER UNITED WIN AGAIN

EXAM FOCUS

EXAM TIP 14

One of three things

The focus of the open cloze task in Part 2 is grammar (whereas the focus of the multiple-choice cloze in Part 1 is mainly vocabulary). You will often have to deal with things such as modal and auxiliary verbs. If you find a space between a modal or auxiliary verb and the main verb, then the missing word could be one of three things: some part of the verb phrase (**be**, **being**, **been** or **have**), a negative (**not**, **never**, etc.) or some kind of adverb (**soon**, **also**, **quickly**, etc.).

1 Open cloze

Read the text below and think of the word which best fits each space. Use only *one* word in each space.

The Internet

It's the coming of age of the Internet – the worldwide network of computers (1) .... offers instantaneous access to practically everything from documents in the British Library to daily newspapers and shopping malls. Use of the technology is exploding all over the world even (2) .... it reaches a mass market (which is just about to happen).

The Internet (3) .... almost certainly be the 20th century's greatest technological invention, comparable to, and maybe exceeding, the importance of electricity and printing (though without (4) .... these discoveries the Internet (5) .... not exist).

The possibilities for the development of the technology are almost without limit. Technology already exists which links the computer (6) .... the television set. To prove it means business, one TV company is immediately ordering a million 'set-top boxes' enabling existing TV sets to receive all the new Internet facilities. This alone, however, (7) .... not guarantee success. There are plenty of other competitors and they will soon (8) .... joined by others.

We will have (9) .... get used not just to everyday items (10) .... sold through the Internet but a new generation of digital products, including magazines and films, which can (11) .... reproduced and sent down telephone lines at (12) .... extra cost to the producer.

(adapted from Victor Keegan, 'What a Web we Weave', *The Guardian*)

2 Error correction

Read the text below and look carefully at each line. Some of the lines are correct, and some have a word which should not be there. If a line is correct, put a tick by it. If a line has a word which should not be there, write the word at the end of the line. There are two examples at the beginning (0 and 00).

The competition

0   The national championships are in two months. I'll have been in a hard   *a*

00 training for just over fourteen weeks by then. When I say hard, I mean it.   ✓

1   I estimate that I will have been done about four and a half thousand laps

2   of the track in my fourteen week training period. Young athletes from all

3   over the country will be attending, all of whom will, such like me, be hoping

4   to impress the national coaches. I've been thinking about what I am going

5   to do before the races will start. People say you have to put the crowd and

6   other competitors out of your mind. You are supposed so to focus on warming

7   up but I want to remember every face. Coaches tell you not to think about

8   winning, just running – but I'm going to do. My parents are going to be there

9   to watch me. I hope I'll be able to do my best because of their help has been

10 so important and I would really like to make them proud of me. I won't know

11 until the next week when we start timing my runs seriously what chance of

12 winning shall I have. My friends say that I am an optimist and, even though

13 it will be being my first time at a big competition such as this, I think that I

14 can likely get one of the first three places. This would be good enough for

15 me to be considered for selection for the national team before the end of the

     year.

Unit 12 **Prepositions**

Language focus: prepositions of place, movement and time; other prepositional phrases
Exam focus: open cloze and multiple-choice cloze questions

LEAD-IN

In Unit 6 we looked at dependent prepositions where adjectives like *rude*, and verbs like *depend* were seen to be followed by certain prepositions: *rude to* and *depend on*.

Prepositions are also common in structures called prepositional phrases. These are phrases where a preposition is used with another word, most commonly a noun. In these phrases the use of the preposition is related more to the word following the preposition rather than the word preceding it.

*I'd seen the man **at the window** before.*
*They got **in the car** and left.*

Working with another student, look at the ways Students A and B have recorded prepositional phrases. Then put the following prepositions in the room as Student A would do, and the prepositional phrases you are thinking of on the cards like Student B.

on   in   at   by   out of

Student A

98

Student B

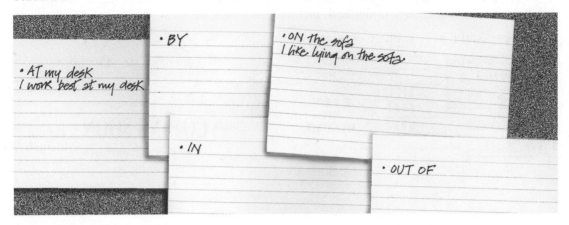

REFERENCE

Sections A–D below cover the most commonly confused prepositions of place, movement and time.

A *Place:* in, at, on

1. **In** is mainly used with the meaning of 'inside something'.
   The knife is in the box in the kitchen drawer.

   In is also used when talking about places as areas: towns, cities, countries, etc.
   We live in Augsburg, which is in southern Germany.

2. **At** is used to talk about the location of something when the location is understood as a point rather than a surface or enclosed space.
   I saw her face at the window.

   At is also used when talking about public places or institutions: shops, public facilities, addresses, etc.
   Several demonstrators are being held at the police station.

   At is also used when talking about places as stopping points on a journey somewhere.
   This train doesn't stop at either Winchurch or Barnhurst.

3. **On** is used mainly when talking about surfaces: walls, tables, floors, etc.
   Don't hang the picture on the wall until I've dusted it.

   On is also used when talking about a place we think of as being in the shape of a line, e.g. a road, a river, a coast.
   What's the speed limit on a British motorway?

   NOTE: After verbs of movement when the idea is 'going from one place to another' we usually use the preposition **to**.
   The last time I went to Hong Kong was in 1984. (not: *in Hong Kong*)

1 Working with another student, discuss where you would find the following signs and labels. Write your answer under each picture.

Example: WIPE YOUR FEET *on a doormat*

WIPE YOUR FEET ←	VISITING FANS ONLY	BABY ON BOARD	Don't feed the animals	COMING SOON	6 SIDE A	7 SIZE 45	8 Do not disturb
1	2	3	4	5			

1 ....   5 ....

2 ....   6 ....

3 ....   7 ....

4 ....   8 ....

B *Movement:* off, into, onto, out of, over, under, down from, towards, away from, round

Complete your own reference section for these prepositions by matching them to the pictures in Exercise 2.

2 Working with another student, decide which preposition you would need to use to describe the movements of the cat in the picture below.

Example: *Picture 1 – into.*

C *Time:* in, at, on

3 Complete the table below by writing down one or two examples for each category and writing in the correct preposition in each box. Look at the examples already done for you.

Times	....	five o'clock / ....
Parts of the day	....	....
Days	....	weekdays ....
Dates	....	....
Weekends and public holidays	....	....
Months	....	....
Seasons	....	....
Years	....	the sixties / 1945 ....
Centuries	....	....

EXCEPTIONS: **Which preposition would you use with:**

1 .... night?   2 .... Thursday evening?

D *Other prepositional phrases*

There are many other prepositional phrases in English which do not follow any particular pattern. As a learner, you need to spot a particular phrase and then work out how it is used.

4 Look at the chart below. Complete each box with the preposition that can be used with all the words in the box.

.... cash danger the dark public	.... duty the phone the stairs the way
.... home the foot of the moment work	.... chance cheque myself post
.... a ride a walk now the time being	.... breath control danger order

Now put the words below into the correct box in the chart above.

least	the past	holiday	mistake	bounds	silence	a joke	luck
accident	ages	date	a bad mood	strike	once	last	heart
my own	shorts	sight	purpose	respect	a diet	a change	war

5 Complete the sentences with phrases from the box you have just completed above.

1 We stumbled about for a few minutes .... before finding the light.

2 I'm sorry you got so upset. We only hid your keys ....

3 It was no accident. She let the dog out ....

4 We'll either ring you with the results or let you know ....

5 We don't accept cheques without a card. You'll have to pay .... I'm afraid.

6 I'll need to get a new passport before we go. This one is ....

7 We hadn't planned to meet, we just saw each other there ....

8 I saw Chris .... here and gave him a lift home.

COMMUNICATIVE PRACTICE

1 Couch associations

This task is based on the psychological technique of word association: 'I'll say a word and you say the first thing that comes into your head . . . '

Look back at the chart you completed in Exercise 4 and write down eight of the phrases in box A below.

Box A   *Box B*

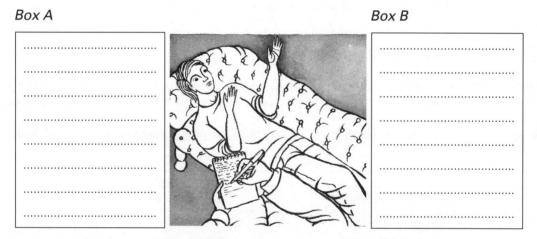

Working with another student, read out the phrases one at a time so that your partner has time to write down *the first word that comes into his/her head* (one word only) in response to each phrase. He/she should write these words in box B of his/her book.

When you have done this, your partner has to read back to you the words he/she has written *in random order* and you have to guess the association. Where an association is not clear to you, ask your partner to explain.

Now change roles so that you fill in box B.

What can you tell about the workings of your partner's mind from this task?

2 Two-joke puzzle

Below are two jumbled jokes. Working with another student, put the parts of the jokes into the correct order and complete the gaps with the appropriate prepositions. Each joke has been started for you.

Joke 1: A policeman was once . . .
Joke 2: A student was once sitting . . .

1 .... duty in town when he noticed a pedestrian holding a piece of string,

2 'Why?' replied his neighbour, without looking up. 'Have you only got nine?'

3 .... a joke he decided to reveal a rather shocking piece of information to the student

4 As this was not the sort of thing people usually do .... public, he asked,

5 .... a library with his books

6 sitting .... the desk next to him.

7 which he was pulling along .... him.

8 'If you look .... the desk for a minute

9 'Why on earth are you pulling that along .... the street?'

10 you'll see we've got 21 toes between us.'

11 'Well,' he replied, 'I thought I'd look stupid trying to push it.'

12 but was not .... a mood to work.

EXAM FOCUS

1 Open cloze

Read the text below and think of the word which best fits each space. Use only *one* word in each space. In line with the focus of this unit, all the missing words here are prepositions.

The Athens Festival

The warmth of the sun (1) .... the Athenian streets hints that summer is right around the corner, and with summer comes the internationally renowned Athens Festival. Every summer since 1955 the experience of watching drama, dance or music (2) .... the foot of the Acropolis (3) .... the open sky has captivated both residents and tourists.

The Athens-based part of the Festival is (4) .... the ancient theatre of Herodes Atticus. It opens (5) .... Sunday 13th June with the Greek National Opera performing Georges Bizet's *Carmen*. Performances continue (6) .... 20th June. Among performers scheduled to appear (7) .... June are Marilyn Horne and the English National Ballet.

Some events have been added to those listed (8) .... the programme, but

organisers expect that even tickets for these additional events will have been sold

(9) .... next Friday. If you're planning to go (10) .... the Festival it is

advisable to check up-to-date programme changes with the Festival office.

(adapted from *Athenscope – The Weekly Guide to What's On in Athens*)

EXAM TIP 15

Look both ways

In the multiple-choice cloze task in Part 1 (as in the open cloze task in Part 2) you have to 'look both ways'. If you need to add a preposition, look at what comes *before* and *after* the space before you choose one.

- If it is a preposition of movement or place then what comes *before*, e.g. the verb, will usually guide your choice.
- If it is a prepositional phrase the word that comes *after* should guide your choice.

2 Multiple-choice cloze

Read the text below and decide which answer A, B, C or D best fits each space.

The dark ocean

As the sun went down, truck after truck reversed down the ramp with bags of cement that

were stacked at the (1) .... of the vehicle deck. (2) .... over the side, Steve

saw the open deck-doors sinking to within a few inches of the water. Caroline was worried

for another (3) ....

All her life she had been (4) .... of boats and the sea because of a recurring

dream. She was treading water (5) .... the dark. She was (6) .... her own.

There were distant lights. She called and called but nobody heard ...

'How does it end?' Steve had asked her.

'I don't know. I always wake up.'

The dream was so vivid that as a schoolgirl Caroline wouldn't even take a boat trip on the

river Thames. Snorkelling with Steve had given her confidence and now she didn't mind boats

as long as it was daylight. But when the *Gurita* finally cast off, it was (7) .... 6.30 pm

and dark.

From the deck Caroline looked through the window into the first-class area. It was

(8) .... with families chatting and playing; a tiny baby snoozed in a hammock.

About halfway through the two-hour journey, the ship suddenly slowed. A seaman

(9) .... his way along the deck giving orders and gesturing – get up and

(10) .... to the other side. Parents sighed as they gathered up children and

luggage. 'This is crazy,' said Steve, 'we'll go inside.'

They found a space and sat on the floor. Caroline's body swayed as she tried to sit

upright. 'Can you feel that?' she asked sharply. The ship was tipping.

Quelling his own rising panic, Steve told her calmly, 'Go outside and get ready to jump.

I'll find some life-jackets.'

(11) .... deck, Caroline was on the high side as the ship tipped. Clutching a

pole for support, she climbed on to the rail. People were (12) .... themselves into

the sea. 'Steve, Steve!' Caroline screamed. 'The bottom of the boat's (13) ....

out of the water – hurry!'

Fighting his way through, Steve glimpsed Caroline in the doorway. He could

(14) .... her in a couple of steps. But the door was rising to the vertical. The

open doorway swung over his head. Caroline disappeared out of (15) ....

(adapted from John Dyson, 'Nightmare on a Dark Ocean', *Reader's Digest*)

1	A middle	B back	C floor	D shelves
2	A Viewing	B Noticing	C Seeing	D Looking
3	A point	B time	C reason	D matter
4	A alarmed	B worried	C anxious	D frightened
5	A in	B on	C by	D at
6	A at	B by	C on	D for
7	A around	B at	C on	D sharp
8	A full	B packed	C contained	D covered
9	A pushed	B got	C moved	D marched
10	A move	B transport	C wait	D be
11	A On	B In	C At	D By
12	A falling	B jumping	C taking	D throwing
13	A getting	B coming	C sinking	D going
14	A fetch	B reach	C make	D arrive
15	A control	B sight	C bounds	D vision

Unit 13 Modals 2

Language focus: uses of modal verbs for speculation and deduction about the past and to talk about obligation and necessity in the past

Exam focus: open cloze and key-word transformation questions

LEAD-IN

1 Look at Picture 1 and discuss the following questions with another student.

1 What do you think the man is going into the shop to buy?
2 How long do you think it will take him?

Picture 1

Now look at Picture 2. Working with another student, discuss what has happened.

Picture 2

2 Now discuss your views on each of the following questions using the language in the box.

couldn't have	must have	may have	could have	might not have
		+ past participle		

1 What happened to the car?
2 Was the woman by the tree involved in the car's disappearance? If so, how?
3 How about the man at the bus stop?
4 And the woman with the pram?
5 Is it possible that the other person in the picture wasn't what he / she seemed?

REFERENCE

Form

must   can('t)   could(n't)   may (not)   mightn't
should(n't)   ought(n't) to   needn't   + have + past participle

NOTES:

1 These forms cover both past simple and present perfect meanings.
   You can't have seen him earlier. (I don't believe you saw him earlier.)
   You can't have seen him already. (I don't believe you've seen him already.)

2 These forms do *not* exist in English: **didn't might, didn't should, mustn't have** + past participle.

A *Speculation and deduction about the past*

In Unit 2 we looked at how the modals **can, may, might, must, could, should** and **ought to** are used to talk about possibility, probability and certainty in the present and future. Here we shall look at how these modals are used to talk about the same ideas in the past.

Look at the table and write down how you express each form in your own language.

Must have expresses the speaker's certainty that something has happened.	*If he's not here by now he **must have** got lost.*	....
Could / may / might have express the idea that there is a possibility that something has happened.	*'He's very late. He **could have** missed the train.'* *'Or it **might have been** delayed.'*	....
Can't / couldn't have express the speaker's certainty that something has not happened.	*My father **can't have taken** the car; his keys are still here.*	....
May not / might not have express the idea that it is possible that something did not happen.	*No one's home. They **might not have received** the letter and **may not have been expecting** us.*	....
Should / ought to have can express the idea that:		
i) you expect something has happened but don't know;	*They **should have found** the message by now. I expect they'll ring soon.*	....
ii) you expected something to happen but it didn't.	*I'm not waiting much longer. She **should have been** here hours ago.*	....

NOTE: **Can have . . .** is only used in questions.
Can she have found out about our plan, do you think?

1 Complete each of the sentences with one of the modal verbs from the box below. Use all the verbs at least once.

should	couldn't	might not	must	could	ought to	can't

1 The car .... have been there to meet us. They promised it would be.

2 She .... have thought we were out. That's why she left a message.

3 .... Jeff have helped you? Didn't you ask him?

4 The package .... have arrived by now but I expect it's stuck in Customs.

5 They .... have seen the message; they would have rung if they had.

6 The police suspect that the couple .... have been using their real names.

7 She .... have gone away for the weekend but I doubt it.

8 Sue .... have bought any food this weekend. The fridge is absolutely empty.

9 Where do you think they .... have hidden the money?

10 You look great. You .... have had a really good time.

B *Obligation and necessity in the past*

In Unit 2 we also looked at how the modals **must, have to, should, ought to** and **needn't** are used to talk about obligation and necessity in the present or future. Here we shall look at how we use modals to talk about obligation and necessity in the past.

Needn't have + the past participle means that someone did something unnecessarily.	*You **needn't have paid** for a hotel. There's plenty of room here.* *We **needn't have gone** in fancy dress. Most people just wore their normal clothes.*
Didn't need to + the infinitive means that something was unnecessary, but it does not tell us if someone did this thing or not.	*He **didn't need to take** the medicine.* (It wasn't necessary to take it, but we don't know if he actually did.)
Didn't have to + the infinitive is similar to **didn't need to**, but is used more when the obligation comes from other people.	*The guard told us we **didn't have to wait** outside – we could go straight in.*
Should have + the past participle expresses the speaker's criticism of what someone has done.	*You **shouldn't have spoken** to him like that. It was very rude of you.*

2 Match either sentence (a) or (b) to the explanation on the right. Only one combination makes sense.

1 a) Rick didn't have to go to the meeting.
   b) Rick needn't have gone to the meeting.   The meeting was a waste of time.

2 a) Maria didn't have to stay at home.
   b) Maria needn't have stayed at home.   So she went out with a friend.

3 a) Simon didn't need to spend his money.
   b) Simon needn't have spent his money.   He got everything free.

4 a) Tina didn't need to do the homework.
   b) Tina didn't have to do the homework.   Her teacher made her, though.

COMMUNICATIVE PRACTICE

1 A moment in sport

Discuss with another student some of the kinds of sports the following words are used with:

match   tournament   race   meeting

Now look at pictures 1–8. With another student, first decide which sport is involved in each picture and then try and explain what has happened in each picture. You need to work out which piece of sporting action the photographer has caught.

Example:

A: *She's obviously a skier.*
B: *Yes, and she must have just turned. Look at the snow.*
A: *Yes, or she could have just stopped.*
B: *No, there's too much snow.*

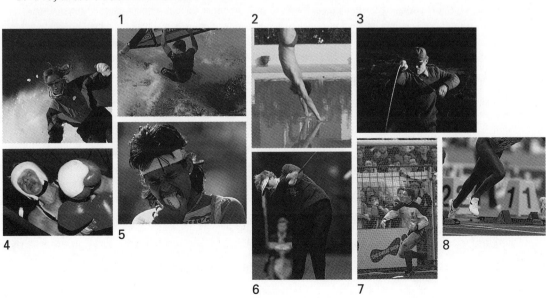

2 What could they have meant?

English is an international language, which means that often people need to translate signs or instructions into English for foreign residents or travellers. Unfortunately, translators do not always manage to express what they intend.

Look at the following 'English' signs and notices that have appeared abroad and working with another student, try and work out what they must have wanted to say.

1 Please leave your values at the front desk. (*In a Paris hotel elevator.*)
2 In case of fire, do your utmost to alarm the porter. (*In a Viennese hotel.*)
3 Stop: Drive sideways. (*A detour sign in Kyushi Japan.*)
4 We take your bags and send them in all directions. (*In a Copenhagen airline ticket office.*)
5 Special today: no ice-cream (*In a Swiss mountain inn.*)
6 Visitors are expected to complain at the office between the hours of 9 and 11 a.m. daily. (*In an Athens hotel.*)
7 Our wines leave you nothing to hope for. (*On the menu of a Swiss restaurant.*)
8 Here speeching American. (*In a Majorcan shop.*)

(from a list compiled by *Addison-Wesley*)

EXAM FOCUS

1 Open cloze

Read the text below and think of the word which best fits each space. Use only *one* word in each space.

The story of a skeleton

In 1984 a team began unearthing the nearly complete skeleton of a twelve-year-old boy who died 1.54 million years ago near Lake Turkana in northern Kenya. The skeleton, named the Turkana boy, is stored in boxes at the National Museum in Nairobi.

The first box held the boy's skull. His teeth and jaws are smaller than the strong, crushing mouth of his predecessors. A meat-eater, Turkana boy (1) .... not need the powerful jaws they used for grinding coarse vegetation and cracking nuts. 'An adult Homo erectus had a brain the size of a one-year-old modern human's,' says Alan Walker, a member of the team which excavated the skeleton. 'Still his brain was twice as large as a chimpanzee's, so he (2) .... have been very clever for his time.'

The real novelty of the Turkana boy, according to Walker, lies below the neck. The length of the thighbone suggests that he (3) .... have stood five feet three inches tall when he died and would have grown to six feet or more (4) .... adulthood, making erectus by far the tallest hominid species to (5) .... evolved by that time.

Examining the limb bones of the Turkana boy, I (6) .... imagine him racing across the savannah, but the vacant eye sockets made me wonder whether we (7) .... have connected as fellow humans. (8) .... we have communicated? Some scientists believe that erectus had basic language, since their increasingly complex social organisation would probably not have (9) .... possible with mere grunts.

Walker argues that Turkana boy's spinal cord (10) .... not have carried enough nerves to enable him to control his breathing as well as modern humans. Linking words into long sentences (11) .... have been impossible.

Yet Homo erectus (12) .... not have been the first explorer after all. Controversial new evidence has some scientists convinced that an older Homo species appeared in Asia just as erectus was emerging in Africa.

(adapted from Rick Gore, 'The Dawn of Humans', *National Geographic*)

2 Key-word transformation

Decide with another student which key-word you need for each sentence from the box below and then complete the second sentence so that it has a similar meaning to the first sentence. You must use between two and five words, including the key-word. There may be more than one correct answer. Remember that contractions count as two words.

must	should	may	need	could	ought to	can't	might	needn't

1 It's possible she lost our address, I suppose.

She .... our address, I suppose.

2 I'm sure she didn't have any idea about the surprise.

She .... idea about the surprise.

3 I expected him to be here hours ago. Where is he?

He .... hours ago. Where is he?

4 Perhaps she didn't know the dialling code for the area.

She .... the dialling code for the area.

5 I presume he took the car keys with him. He usually does.

He .... the car keys with him. He usually does.

6 There was no need for her to take her passport so she left it at the hotel.

She .... her passport so she left it at the hotel.

7 She went to all that trouble for nothing because her friends didn't come.

She .... to all that trouble because her friends didn't come.

8 I expect she's passed her exams, but we'll know next week for sure.

She .... her exams, but we'll know next week for sure.

Unit 14 **The passive**

Language focus: uses of passive; the 'agent' in passive sentences; causative structure: **to have something done**

Exam focus: key-word transformation and open cloze questions

LEAD-IN

1 In a passive sentence the person / thing doing the action is often not mentioned. This person / thing is called *the agent*.

Example: *Your arm will have **to be** bandaged properly.*
Probable agent: A doctor or a nurse.

Read the newspaper extracts below and discuss with another student who or what the probable agent is in each case, or whether the agent is unknown.

Debt drove man to crime   1

A man who planned an armed robbery to solve debt problems *was jailed* at the Old Bailey for 30 months yesterday.

Sheep flock to art gallery   2

Five sheep form part of an art exhibition opening next Thursday. The sheep which *have been* temporarily *coloured* will be at a gallery in Bond Street. The work is by Menashe Kadishman, an Israeli sculptor and former shepherd.

(from the *Independent*)

4,000 Ford jobs to go   3

FORD announced the loss of 4,000 jobs yesterday at the same time as the first Toyota *to be built* in Britain came off the production line.

Most senior citizen   4

DAISY ADAMS, of Church Gresley, Derbyshire, who *is believed* to be Britain's oldest person, celebrated her 113th birthday yesterday.

Accidental blaze

A fire which swept through a hostel in the North German town of Emstek *was* probably *started* accidentally, police said yesterday.   5

(from the *Guardian*)

2 Look back at the extracts in Task 1 and say why you think the agent was not mentioned in each case. Choose from these reasons:

A The agent is probably not known.
B The agent is obvious from the context.
C The agent is too vague to mention.
D The agent has already been or is likely to be mentioned later.

Match the explanations with the extracts.

REFERENCE

A *The passive*

1 Complete each sentence with an appropriate form of the verb *to be* and then match each
verb to one of the tenses a–h below.

1 I can't leave the house at the moment because our new carpet .... fitted.

2 The rubbish .... collected every Thursday morning.

3 The Treaty of Versailles .... signed in 1918.

4 As I entered the room, I had the feeling that I .... watched.

5 We had no idea that our luggage .... put on another plane already.

6 No decision .... taken about the vacant post yet.

7 If no one comes, all these preparations .... made for nothing.

8 The package .... sent to you by courier first thing tomorrow, I promise.

a) present perfect   d) past continuous   g) present continuous
b) past simple   e) present simple   h) future perfect
c) future simple   f) past perfect

Uses

1 The passive is used:

a when it is not necessary to mention the doer of the action (the agent), e.g. in scientific experiments, or when the agent is not known.

*The experiment **has to be done** in controlled conditions.*
*Your seats **must have been double-booked**.*

b very often in texts because of a change of focus between sentences.

*A man in the crowd took out a gun and started firing. Four shots **were fired** altogether.*
The subject of the second sentence is connected to the object of the first sentence.

c in impersonal signs and notices and when talking about rules which apply to everybody:

*Passengers **are not allowed** on the upper deck.*
*Smoking **is forbidden** whilst moving around the plane.*

2 Match each piece of information below to the place in a–h where you are most likely to find it.

1 Contents should be kept in a dry place at all times.	a) a plane
2 Only to be pulled in an emergency.	b) a television screen
3 To be continued . . .	c) a table
4 Pieces must be moved in a clockwise direction.	d) a door
5 Electricity can be generated in a number of ways.	e) a textbook
6 Rooms must be vacated by 12.00.	f) a packet
7 Reserved.	g) a bill
8 You risk being cut off without further notice.	h) instructions for a board game

2 Special uses of the passive in impersonal phrases

We often use the passive when talking about what people generally **say, think, believe** or **know**.

Two different types of passive structure are possible:
Active: *People say that the Prime Minister is about to resign.*
Passive: ***It is said that** the Prime Minister is about to resign.*
Passive: *The Prime Minister **is said to be** about to resign.*

A similar use of the passive can be seen in the phrase *it is not known whether*.

***It is not known whether** the explosion was caused by a bomb.*

Where the action has already taken place, we use a perfect infinitive.
*The Prime Minister is believed **to have resigned**.*

B *Causative structure:* to have something done

> There are certain actions that we do not typically or always perform ourselves. Instead, these actions are usually performed for us by professionals or specialists. To talk about such actions we can use the following structure:
> 'have + object + past participle'.
> *We're going to **have the car serviced** before we go on holiday.*
> *He's **had his hair cut** so short that I hardly recognised him.*

3 Write down two things that people typically have done in the following places.

Example: *At the dry-cleaner's you can have your clothes cleaned.*

1 the dentist's   3 the optician's   5 the hairdresser's
2 the shoe repairer's 4 a garage   6 the beautician's

COMMUNICATIVE PRACTICE

1 Fact triangles

The box below contains information about the people, places and things on the left.

Working with another student, find three relevant pieces of information for each subject. Connect the three pieces of information by drawing a triangle and then make sentences using the information, and the passive.

Example: *The Acropolis is made of marble.*
              was built in 500 B.C.
              was used as a temple.

1 John F. Kennedy

2 Napoleon

3 Australia

4 The Olympic Games

5 The First World War

6 Motion pictures

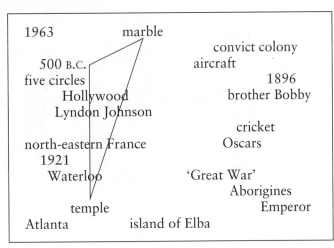

```
1963              marble
                          convict colony
     500 B.C.             aircraft
   five circles                  1896
      Hollywood           brother Bobby
      Lyndon Johnson

                                 cricket
north-eastern France     Oscars
   1921
     Waterloo            'Great War'
                           Aborigines
                              Emperor
        temple
  Atlanta      island of Elba
```

2 We've had everything done

Look at the two pictures of the house below *before* and *after* the Robinson family had everything done. Working with another student, discuss all the things the Robinsons have had done.

Example: *They've had new wallpaper put up.*

Then list the different people the Robinsons have paid to do the work. Write the different occupations in the box below.

Picture 1: Before

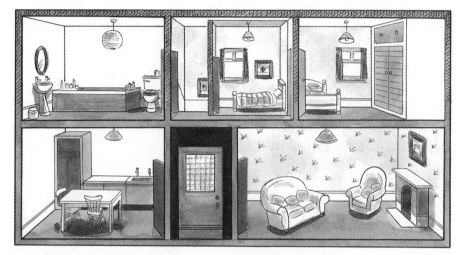

Picture 2: After

EXAM FOCUS

EXAM TIP 16

Check the tense

Typical 'passive' transformations in
Part 3 involve changing an active form
to a passive form or a passive form to an
active form. Remember, however, to be
consistent in the use of tenses between
the two sentences.

1 Key-word transformation

Complete the second sentence so that it has a similar meaning to the first sentence, using
the word given. Do not change the word given. You must use between two and five
words, including the word given.

Example: I am sure someone was watching me.
I am sure I was being watched. **was**

1 People say that inflation is getting out of control.

Inflation .... getting out of control. **be**

2 Our water heater was repaired last week by the plumber you recommended.

We .... last week by the plumber you recommended. **had**

3 We'll have finished all the decorating by the weekend.

All the decorating .... by the weekend. **been**

4 The car ought to be looked at by a mechanic.

You .... at by a mechanic. **should**

5 I hate it when people criticise me at work.

I hate .... work. **being**

6 Someone should have informed her about the delay.

She .... informed about the delay. **ought**

7 The customs official made us empty out our suitcases.

We .... out our suitcases. **were**

8 The council is planning to build a new car park here.

A new car park .... here by the council. **going**

9 The descendants of the Mina tribe still inhabit the island.

The island .... by descendants of the Mina tribe. **is**

10 No one knows whether there are any survivors.

It .... whether there are any survivors. **not**

EXAM TIP 17

Passive – or not?

In completing the open cloze task in Part 2 you may need to decide whether or not a sentence involves a passive form. For example,

'He was .... to keep quiet' could be completed with **made** (passive form) or **right** (adjective).

'She .... not asked about anything' could be completed with **was** (passive) or **has** (active).

Thinking carefully about the context of the sentence in the passage should help you to make your choice.

2 Open cloze

Read the text below and think of the word which best fits each space. Use only *one* word in each space.

Sheep on the road!

A busy Dutch city is planning to introduce live sheep to its roads (1) .... an obstacle to speeding. Culembourg struck on the bizarre solution to its traffic problems after studying the experiences of drivers (2) .... Britain's country roads. 'It's impossible to speed past the sheep if you drive in the Yorkshire Dales,' Chris De Bakker, a city councillor spokesman, said.

The project will involve five or six sheep (3) .... released onto roads plagued (4) .... speeding motorists. (5) .... successful, the number of sheep will (6) .... increased to more than 100. Cattle-grids are (7) .... installed to keep the sheep from wandering off designated areas to busier roads where they (8) .... face certain death. The council last week insisted that the project was 'absolutely serious'. But it (9) .... come in for heavy criticism from animal lovers who fear carnage on the roads.

It is not the first time Culembourg (10) .... gone back to nature to solve a problem. An earlier project involved replacing lawn-mowers with a force of 40 sheep and ten cows to keep municipal grass short.

The life expectancy of the first woolly speeding bumps has yet (11) .... be established, but animal rights activists agree the creatures will be in grave peril. In Scotland and Yorkshire there is a tradition that the Dutch planners may be unaware of. Certain locals have (12) .... known to target sheep with their cars, aiming to carry off a year's free supply of chops in their boot.

(adapted from Jane Szita, 'Say Baa Baa to Bad Driving', *The Sunday Times*)

Unit 15 Word formation

Language focus: meanings of prefixes and suffixes with adjectives, verbs and nouns
Exam focus: word formation questions

LEAD-IN

A lot of words in English can be said to be related to each other because they contain the same root word, e.g. *clean – reclean – cleaner*. We usually think of a word like *clean* as the root word and the other words as being formed by adding prefixes or suffixes to it.

Prefixes indicate changes in meaning but do not usually indicate a change in the part of speech of the word, e.g. *clean* (v) – *reclean* (v); clean (adj) – *unclean* (adj).

Suffixes usually indicate a different part of speech, e.g. *clean* (adj or v) – *cleaner* (n) – *cleanliness* (n).

1 Look at the headlines 1–6 and the extracts a–f below. Match each headline to an extract.

1 Washington party over-priced and over-crowded

2 **Misdialled phone call 'led to attack by doctor'**

3 **BEATLES FOR CENTRAL PARK REUNION**

4 **Young giants of Japan outgrow weakling image**

5 **Police detain 107 illegal immigrants**

6 **'Healing Priest' last hope for incurably ill**

a   Miss B said that she found herself speaking to Dr Courtney by chance

(from the *Independent*)

b   The source was quoted as saying the concert was being backed by "an extremely wealthy, eccentric American".

c   He said three other men were found hiding on the roof of the lift.

(from the *Star*)

d   There have already complaints that the organisers have oversold, with many people grumbling that they have received nothing for the money that they have handed out.

e   The legs of today's 17- to 18-year-old boys are 3.8 centimetres longer than those of their fathers at the same age,

(from the *Guardian*)

f   Tales of cures for cancer, arthritis and other illnesses have earned Father Corsie Legaspi a church dispensation to set up a unique "healing ministry" to accommodate a growing number of believers.

2 The table below gives several prefixes. Find examples of words using these prefixes in the headlines above and write them in the *Examples* column. Next to each word write the part of speech it is: (n), (v), (adj) or (adv). Then complete the *Meaning* column with one of these meanings:

not   too much   bad(ly) or wrong   better / more than   again

Prefixes	Examples	Meaning
il-		
mis-		
over-		
in-		
re-		
out-		

REFERENCE

A *Adjectives*

1 The following prefixes all give the meaning of **not** when added to an adjective.

dis-   il-   im-   in-   ir-   un-

Example: *That was **unfair** of you.* (**not** fair of you)

1 Match one of the prefixes in point 1 above to the words below.

1 loyal   4 honest   7 common   10 experienced
2 reliable   5 regular   8 polite   11 patient
3 legal   6 sincere   9 responsible   12 logical

2 The following suffixes can be added to a root word to form adjectives.

-al   -ful   -less   -ous   -y

Example: *You mustn't be so care**less** with money.*

2 Use one of the suffixes in point 2 to make the adjective forms of the words below.

1 music   4 courage   7 success   10 advantage
2 risk   5 thought   8 danger   11 rust
3 help   6 stress   9 sleep   12 accident

NOTE: Some adjectives, such as **careful,** form the opposite with -less, e.g. **careless.** Some, such as **successful,** form the opposite with **un-,** e.g. **unsuccessful.**

Which of the adjectives you have just formed can be contrasted like this?

---

3 Other common adjectival endings are: **-ive, -ent, -able** and **-ic.** These endings are not simply added to the root words; the root itself is changed slightly when one of these endings is added.

Examples: *I am not particularly **confident** about the result.* (root word: **confidence**)
*He's quite an **aggressive** character.* (root word: **aggression**)

4 Many verbs have past and present participle forms which can be used as adjectives. For example **to tire: tired / tiring.** The **-ing** adjective form is used to talk about the general quality of the thing we are discussing.
*He's a really **boring** speaker. I hope I don't fall asleep.*

The **-ed** adjective form describes a person's reaction or response to the thing being discussed.
*She quickly became **bored** with the lecture and left.*

---

3 **Complete each sentence with the correct form of the word given in brackets.**

1 I found his new book really ....   (interest)

2 Most people left the concert feeling ....   (dissatisfy)

3 Hasn't he become .... since he started that job? He talks about nothing else.   (bore)

4 The children felt so .... about opening the presents that it took ages to get them to sleep.   (excite)

5 I thought she had some very .... arguments.   (convince)

6 Your new friend kept us .... all afternoon.   (amuse)

7 The person I sit next to just doesn't stop chatting which is .... if you're trying to work.   (annoy)

8 That's a film I don't particularly want to see. I've heard it's really .... (depress)

B Verbs

---

1 Common verb prefixes are:

dis-	mis-	out-	over-	re-	under-

---

4 Discuss with another student the kinds of meaning these prefixes have when used with verbs. Then complete each sentence using one of the prefixes above, together with the verb at the end of the sentence.

Example: *Hotels on the island will soon be reopening after the winter break.* OPEN

1 I'm sorry I'm late but the car .... in the traffic. HEAT

2 The captain is in trouble again for .... an order. OBEY

3 The prisoner is claiming that he was .... whilst in police custody. TREAT

4 I'll never be able to eat all this. I think we've .... ORDER

5 In the new plan, the library will be .... to another building. LOCATE

6 My team was completely .... by the opposition. PLAY

7 I .... him because he has lied to us before. TRUST

8 The repairs cost almost double what I thought they would. I really

.... how much damage was done. ESTIMATE

2 Two common verb endings are **-en** and **-ise**.

-en is added to several adjectives and some nouns to give the verb form. Verbs formed in this way have the meaning of 'to make more . . .', e.g. **weaken**: 'to make weaker'. Other examples are:

harden	soften	sharpen	tighten	loosen	shorten	sweeten
frighten	lengthen	strengthen				

-ise is also a common verb ending. This ending is not simply added to the noun form; the noun itself is changed slightly when this ending is added, e.g.

sympathise	fantasise	dramatise	civilise	prioritise

C Nouns

1 Common endings for general or abstract nouns are:

-ity	-ness	-ment	-sion	-tion	-ism	-ing

*After a few weeks at the school my feeling of **loneliness** began to disappear.*

2 Common endings for personal nouns (nouns indicating people) are: **-er**, **-or** and **-ist**. *Napoleon adopted the title of Emper**or** of France.*

5 Complete the following table with the correct nouns and verbs.

General noun	Personal noun	Verb
....	....	entertain
interpretation	....	....
....	....	manage
....	....	employ
....	typist	....
....	....	demonstrate
invention	....	....
....	....	compete

COMMUNICATIVE PRACTICE

1 Interpreting luggage

We can often tell something about people by the kinds of things they take with them on holiday. With another student, discuss the items and the titles of books that the four people below are taking with them and decide what sort of person you think each one is.

Thinking about the meaning of the highlighted prefixes and suffixes should help you identify each person.

PERSON A

- **re**chargeable batteries
- **un**leaded petrol vouchers
- **re**cycled writing paper
- *The **Dis**appearing Earth*

PERSON B

- sugar**less** biscuits
- coffee sweet**ener**
- **non**-fattening cheese
- ***Over**eating*

PERSON C

- **un**marked essays
- **in**visible correction fluid
- **over**due library books
- *Children's **Mis**behaviour*

PERSON D

- **un**finished reports
- **in**complete accounts
- **un**answered letters
- *How to **Un**wind*

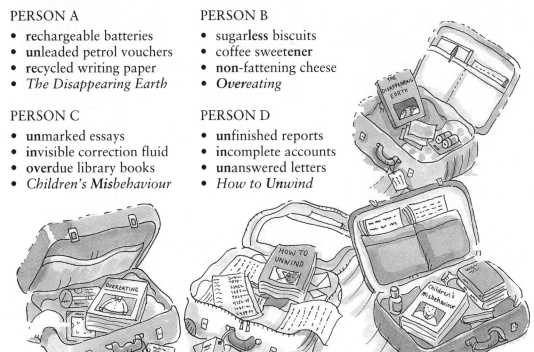

2 Situating signs

Look at the signs below and, working with another student, work out exactly where you might find them. Think carefully about the meaning of the prefixes.

EXAM FOCUS

EXAM TIP 18

Two types of knowledge

The word formation task in Part 5 requires you to spot:

* The *part of speech* that is needed in each space – a noun, verb, adjective or adverb – and to think about the spelling of this word in connection to the word you are given.

* Whether you need to change this word *grammatically* to make it fit the sentence (make it plural, add a past tense ending, and a negative prefix, etc.).

1 Word formation

a Use the word given in capitals at the end of each line to form a word that fits in the space in the same line. There is an example at the beginning (0).

Weird newspaper stories

From the earliest days of newspaper (0) .p̲u̲b̲l̲i̲s̲h̲i̲n̲g̲., the serious affairs   PUBLISH

of the nation have generated pages of print. But while (1) ....   PASSION

debated issues of the past probably only interest (2) .... today,   HISTORY

early newspapers also found space to record more off-beat events: a death by lightning or some remarkable (3) .... case. The fascination of these   MEDICINE

types of stories is eternal.

    Weird tales often only appeared as snippets – like the story of a man who was

found (4) .... to death, standing upright in a ditch. But other stories   FREEZE

gripped the (5) .... Nineteenth-century readers were haunted by   IMAGINE

(6) .... reports of cannibalism on the raft of the Medusa just as readers   LENGTH

this century have been fascinated by accounts of the Andes (7) ....   SURVIVE

    The weird combines both the familiar and the (8) .... A   EXPECT

newsman once defined the (9) .... between the newsworthy and   DIFFER

the uninteresting – his remark serves just as well to define the weird: 'When

a dog bites a man, that is not news. But when a man bites a dog, that is news.'

(adapted from the (10) .... to *Strange but True – the world's weirdest*   INTRODUCE

newspaper stories)

b Use the word given in capitals at the end of each line to form a word that fits in the space in the same line. There is an example at the beginning (0).

The Greek islands

There are about 2,000 Greek islands and every year more (0) ...*tourists*... visit   TOUR

them – to study the past, sail from island to island, marvel at the (1) .... ,   ARCHITECT

bask in the heat or bathe amid incomparable (2) .... Fortunately, many   SCENE

of the islands are still (3) .... Nowhere else has the same heady,   SPOIL

(4) .... appeal for both young and old. Lawrence Durrell lived in the   FORGET

Greek islands for many years, and the early fruits of his (5) .... , books   ATTACH

such as *Bitter Lemons* and *Prospero's Cell*, are famous.

    This book is a guide, but a very (6) .... one, which weaves together   PERSON

(7) .... , history and myth, architectural and archaeological study and   DESCRIBE

memories. The beautiful (8) .... , many in colour, add an extra   ILLUSTRATE

dimension to the text. It is a book to treasure for anybody who has been to

the Greek islands or plans to go. It is also a work of literature (9) ....   WORTH

of the talent and (10) .... of the author of the modern classic, *The*   ACHIEVE

Alexandria Quartet.

        (adapted from publicity material for *The Greek Islands*, by Lawrence Durrell)

Unit 16 **Conditional sentences**

Language focus: uses of zero, first, second and third conditional forms; **if** and other
conditional link words

Exam focus: key-word transformation question

LEAD-IN

1 **Below are eight famous quotations which use conditionals. Working with another
student, complete each quotation by matching the first half of the sentence on the left to
the second half on the right.**

1 If those of you in the cheap
  seats clap your hands,

2 If you have nothing to say,

3 If only I had known,

4 If you give me six lines
  written by the most honest
  man,

5 Lady Astor: 'If I were
  married to you, I'd put
  poison in your coffee.'
  Winston Churchill: 'If you
  were my wife,

6 How wonderful opera
  would be

7 Playing Shakespeare is very
  tiring. You never get to sit
  down

a) I'd drink it.'

b) unless you're a king.
   (*Josephine Hall, 1886–1957*)

c) say nothing!
   (*Charles Caleb Colton,
   1780–1832*)

d) I would have become a
   watchmaker.
   (*Oppenheimer, the inventor
   of the atom bomb*)

e) I'll find something in them to
   hang him.
   (*Cardinal de Richelieu,
   1585–1642*)

f) the rest of you can just rattle
   your jewellery.
   (*John Lennon, 1940–1980*)

g) if there were no singers.
   (*Gioacchino Rossini,
   1792–1868*)

2 **The quotations above illustrate four types of conditional sentence. Look back at the
quotations and complete the table below.**

Quotation	If clause	Other clause
1, ...	....	.... or present simple
....	....	**will** + infinitive without **to**
....	past simple tense	....
....	....	**would have** + past participle

REFERENCE

1 Look at the phrases in the box below which describe the main uses of the zero and first conditional forms. Then read Sections A and B and complete sentences 1–3 in each section with the correct phrases from the box.

> giving instructions
> making offers / requests and promises / threats
> talking about things that are always true
> talking about people's typical reactions to situations
> talking about how future situations may develop

A *'Zero' or general conditional*

Form

If + present simple tense, present simple tense imperative

The words **when** and **whenever** can often be substituted for **if** with almost no change in meaning.

Uses

1 This form is often used when: *talking about things that are always true.*
   *White sugar **turns** a horrible black colour if it **is heated**.*
   *Divers **get** dizzy when they **come** up to the surface too quickly.*

2 This form is also used when:
   ....
   *He **gets** upset if I **mention** her name.*
   *If I **don't have** breakfast, I **feel** terrible for the rest of the morning.*

3 The imperative form is used in this structure when:
   ....
   Don't panic if you see a shark while diving.
   *If you get lost, **use** your whistle to call for help.*

B *First conditional*

Form

If + present simple / present continuous tense, **will** + infinitive without **to**

Can / may / could are used instead of **will** to express less certainty:

*We **might** have to start without you if you're late.*

Uses

1 We use this form when:

....

*If we **don't stay** in London, I'll probably have to change jobs.*
*There'll be trouble if Sheila **is coming** with Karen's ex-husband.*

2 This form is also used when:

....

*We **won't** go back to work unless the pay offer **is improved**.*
***Will** you **help** out if we **need** another pair of hands?*
*I'll bring some extra chairs round if you **like**.*

C *Other words and phrases that can link conditional clauses*

Linking word/phrase	Meaning	Example
as long as / provided (that)	. . . but only if	*I'll cook, provided that you wash up.*
in case	to be prepared for the possibility that . . .	*Bring your credit card in case the cashpoint isn't working.*
otherwise	or (else)	*Please hurry, otherwise we'll miss the start.*
suppose	what if . . .	*Suppose she's out – how will we get in?*
unless	if . . . not	*I'll call the police unless you pay.*
whether		*He doesn't know whether to go.* *It's a question of whether we can afford it.*

2 Complete the sentences with a word or phrase from the table in Section C.

1 Don't sit like that .... you'll end up with back problems.

2 I won't go .... the company agrees to pay all expenses.

3 Simon ought to see a doctor .... he'll get worse.

4 .... you run out of money, what then?

5 Take my phone number just .... you need to ring me later.

6 I really can't decide .... it's worth going or not.

7 I'll go with you .... I don't have to do the driving.

8 Wait here a minute .... I'll introduce you to Karen.

D Other present tenses

Use of the present continuous tense, the present perfect tense and the present perfect continuous tense is possible in zero and first conditional sentences.

Go and see a doctor, if you've been getting those headaches.
I'll give you a key in case the bell isn't working again.
If she has had to work late again, I'll be really angry.

3 Look at the phrases in the box below which describe the main uses of the second and third conditional forms. Then read Sections E and F and complete sentences 1–2 in each with the correct phrases from the box.

> talking about imaginary results of past events
> talking about unreal / imaginary situations
> expressing regrets
> talking about less probable or unlikely future situations

E Second conditional

Form

If + past simple / past continuous tense, **would** + infinitive without **to**

Might and **could** can be used instead of **would** when there is more doubt in the speaker's mind.

Uses

1 We use this form when:

....

*It **would** be great if you **could** come but I know time off is a problem.*
*Suppose she **won** the election, do you think she'd keep her promises?*

2 The main use of this form is when:

....

*If there **were** more space here, I'd ask you to stay with us.*
*I **wouldn't** want to live anywhere else even if I **had** all the money in the world.*

NOTE: In such conditional sentences **were** is usually the preferred form of the verb **to be**, though **was** can also be used.

F *Third conditional*

Form

If + past perfect simple / continuous, **would have** + past participle

Uses

1 When we use the third conditional, we are always referring to something that either happened or didn't happen in the past but:

....

*If you **hadn't told** that man you spoke French, he **would** probably **have left** us alone.* (But you did tell him.)

2 This form can have the meaning of:

....

and is commonly used with the phrase **if only** in this sense:

*If only I'd **known** about your offer then, I **wouldn't have taken** this job.*

4 **Complete the sentences by putting an appropriate verb form in each blank. (One, two, three or four words.)**

1 If I .... you were coming, I .... there to meet you at the station.

2 It's unlikely that she .... with us even if we paid for her ticket.

3 If you .... just a few close friends to the party, the place

.... left in the mess it's now in.

4 We .... here much earlier if we .... lost on the way.

5 I .... on a long holiday if I .... you. You look as though you could do with a break.

6 If I .... prime minister at that time, I ....
the same decision.

7 I'm not very optimistic about getting a loan. If you .... a bank

manager .... you lend us the money?

8 If only the trains .... running on time. We ....
missed the first half of the match.

COMMUNICATIVE PRACTICE

1 Body language

Look at the gestures below and discuss with another student what you think they mean.

Example: *If someone makes the gesture in Picture 1, it probably means they . . .*
If someone does this, I think it means . . .

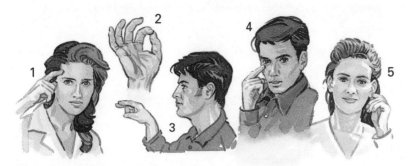

2 How would you get out of . . . ?

Imagine that you are in the three situations described below. Working with at least one other student, decide what you would say or do to get out of trouble.

Situation A

While babysitting for a friend you find a letter to her inside a magazine. It is from another friend and is very personal. You read it but accidentally spill coffee on it.

Situation B

You work in a shop. One Saturday night after closing time you realise you have left your purse or wallet inside and go back to get it, using your keys. When you leave you do not realise you've left your key in the door. That weekend several valuable items are stolen and the police are not sure how the burglars got in. If your boss finds out it was your key, she'll sack you.

Situation C

Your family is preparing a large surprise party for your grandfather's seventieth birthday. You have been given the job of doing the shopping but accidentally leave the enormous shopping list you have prepared somewhere where he sees it. He's very curious about the contents of the list.

Write your group's solution to each situation in large letters on a piece of card.

Example: B: *I'd say my bag had been stolen.*

Your teacher will then put the cards for each situation on the board. Say why your solution would be a better way to get out of the situation than any of the others.

One member of the class should be chosen to act as judge for each situation.

EXAM FOCUS

1 Key-word transformation

a Circle the form of the conditional you think you need to use to complete the sentences below. The numbers relate to the zero (0), first, second and third conditional forms in the Reference section. Then, complete the second sentence so that it has a similar meaning to the first sentence, using the word given. Do not change the word given. You must use between two and five words, including the word given.

1 You only get so depressed because you worry.

   If you .... not get so depressed.   **not**   0 1 2 3

2 The only reason I went was because Stephen was there.

   I .... if Stephen hadn't been there.   **have**   0 1 2 3

3 Would you like me to move my car?

   I .... you like.   **if**   0 1 2 3

4 You're always blaming me for things that go wrong.

   Whenever .... me.   **anything**   0 1 2 3

5 You might be delayed so I won't cook until you get here.

   I won't cook until you get here .... delayed.   **case**   0 1 2 3

6 You don't do any exercise and that's why you put on weight.

   If .... you wouldn't put on weight.   **some**   0 1 2 3

7 I didn't phone because I didn't know you were back.

   I .... I'd known you were back.   **if**   0 1 2 3

8 Going on deck always makes me feel sea-sick.

   I always .... go on deck.   **if**   0 1 2 3

b In the sentences below the difficulty is not in choosing which conditional form to use but how using a different *link word* changes the pattern of the sentence.

1 They're still not sure if they are going to come.

   They still .... they are going to come or not.   **decided**

2 I don't mind driving long distances when the roads are good.

   Driving long distances is fine .... the roads are good.   **as**

3 If you don't put sun cream on, you'll burn.

   You .... sun cream on.   **unless**

4 You should book your seats soon otherwise they'll be sold out.

   They'll be sold out .... your seats soon.   **if**

5 There's a chance it might rain later so bring a coat.

   Bring a coat .... later.   **case**

Unit 17 Verb and sentence patterns

Language focus: verbs followed by the **-ing** form, infinitive with **to**, or **that** clause; reported speech and tense changes; verbs and phrases followed by the infinitive without **to**

Exam focus: key-word transformation question

LEAD-IN

Looking in a good dictionary is usually one of the best ways to find out the kind of sentence pattern that typically follows a particular verb. Often important information is contained in the example sentences given.

Working with another student, complete the table about sentence patterns after verbs by reading the dictionary entries below. Put a ✔ if the sentence pattern can be used and a ✗ if it cannot. Some have been done for you as examples.

Each verb can be followed by at least two different types of sentence pattern.

Finally, use the information in the dictionary entries to find an explanation for the uses of the different patterns with each verb.

1

tell /tel/ v **told** /təʊld/ **1** [T (about, of, to) to make (something) known in words to (someone); express in words: *If you knew you were going to be late, why didn't you tell me?\He's good at telling jokes.\Do you always tell the truth?\Tell me all about your new job.\The boss will have to be told about this.\He told us of his wonderful adventures in foreign lands.* [+obj(i)+obj(d)] *I always tell the children a story/tell a story to the children before they go to bed* [+obj+(that)] *John told us he'd seen you in town.* ... **2** [T] to cause (someone) to know what they must do; order; direct: *That child has got to learn to do what/as he's told* [+obj+wh-] *Don't try to tell me how to behave!* [+obj+to-v] *I told you to get here early, so why are you late?*

(adapted from the *Longman Dictionary of Contemporary English*)

2

(from the *Longman Dictionary of Contemporary English*)

try[1] /traɪ/ v **1** [I;T +to-v; obj] to make an effort or attempt (to do something): *I don't think I can do it, but I'll try.\If you don't succeed the first time, try again.\Don't criticize him too much; he's trying his best/his hardest.\He tried to stand on his head, but he couldn't.\The two sides are still trying to reach an agreement.\Try to get there on time.\I tried hard not to laugh when I saw his new haircut.* **2** (T+v-ing] to attempt and do (something) as a possible way of gaining a desired result: *If the car won't start, try pushing it.*

3

make If you make someone do something, you force them to do it. EG *You've got to make him listen... They were made to sit and wait for two hours.*

    V+O+ INF:IF
    PASS V+*to* INF
    = compel

(from the *Collins COBUILD English Language Dictionary*)

Verb	+ -ing	+ infinitive with to	+ that clause	+ infinitive without to
tell			√	X
make			X	
try				

REFERENCE

A *Verb* + ing

1 These are some common verbs that are followed by the **-ing** form of another verb.

admit	**appreciate**	avoid	can't help	**can't stand**	consider	delay
deny	enjoy	**fancy**	feel like	finish	**hate**	**imagine**	**involve**
keep	love	mention	**mind**	postpone	practise	resist	**risk**
propose	suggest

*You should **avoid taking** the A312 – it's always busy.*
*Haven't you **finished building** the wall yet?*

2 The verbs in bold print in the box above can also be used with the pattern:
'verb + object + **-ing** form'.

*You don't **mind us coming** along, do you?*
*I'll go as long as it doesn't **involve me hanging** around.*
*I can't **imagine not having** a computer at work now.*

NOTE: **Keep** has a different meaning when used with an object.

*He **keeps annoying** us.* (doesn't stop)
*He **kept us waiting** outside.* (made us . . .)

B *Verb* + *infinitive with* to

1 These are some common verbs that are followed by the infinitive with **to**.

afford	agree	allow	appear	arrange	ask	choose
expect	fail	help	hope	learn	manage	offer	pretend
promise	refuse	threaten	want

*How can she **afford to go** on holiday twice a year?*
*We **expect to land** at approximately 1.45 local time.*

2 The following verbs are used with the pattern 'verb + object + infinitive with **to**'.

advise	allow	ask	encourage	expect	force	get	help
intend	invite	leave	order	persuade	prefer	remind	
teach	tell	want	warn				

*The guard only **allowed us to enter** after searching our bags.*
*Can I **remind you** once again **to take** all your belongings with you?*

(For more on object patterns see Unit 9.)

1 Match the parts of the sentences on the left to those on the right to make complete sentences which use the verb patterns described above.

1 I really can't imagine
2 My doctor has advised
3 Could you remind your brother
4 There doesn't appear
5 Some people just can't help
6 You don't fancy
7 Hasn't she arranged
8 People ought to be encouraged
9 The boys consistently denied
10 He really can't stand

a) coming out tonight, I suppose?
b) to do more exercise.
c) people smoking.
d) her leaving without me.
e) me not to go out at all.
f) to be any sign of them.
g) breaking into the car.
h) to be met by someone?
i) to bring the cheque?
j) making fools of themselves.

C *Verb +* -ing *or infinitive with* to

Some verbs can be followed by either the **-ing** form or an infinitive with **to**, usually with some difference in meaning. Some of these are given below in Exercise 2.

2 Look at the examples and explanations. Complete the explanations with either 'infinitive' or '-*ing* form'.

1 **need**

  *I **need to go** to the hairdresser.*
  *My hair **needs cutting** again.*

  a) The .... is used when someone is going to do something.

  b) The .... is used when something is going to be done.

2 **forget** and **remember**

  *Don't **forget to feed** the cat.*
  *I'll never **forget meeting** her.*
  *I don't **remember seeing** him.*
  *I hope you **remembered to feed** the cat.*

  a) The .... is used to talk about past memories.

  b) The .... is used when there is the idea of obligation.

3 **stop**

*We only **stopped to have** lunch.*
*I wish you'd **stop annoying** me.*

a) The .... is used when we mean 'to stop what one is doing'.

b) The .... is used when we mean **stop** 'in order to . . . '.

4 **begin**, **start** and **continue**

*She's **starting to get** tired.*
*We **started winning** halfway through the game.*
*He soon **began to lose** patience.*
*Perhaps we should **continue playing** tomorrow?*

The infinitive and the **-ing** form can both be used with no difference in meaning, but

only the .... is used after verbs in continuous tenses.

5 **try**

*I **tried to get** in but couldn't.*
*Try **ringing** Anne, she'll know.*

a) The .... shows that there is / was / may be some difficulty.

b) The .... shows that something is / should be easy to do.

6 **mean**

*I didn't **mean to hurt** anyone.*
*If it **means travelling** overnight, I'd rather not take the cheaper flight.*

a) The .... is used with the meaning 'involve'.

b) The .... is used with the meaning 'intend'.

D *Verb* + that *clause*

1 Some verbs are typically followed by a **that** clause:

argue	**check**	**complain**	explain	**insist**
say	wish (meaning 'prefer it if')	.		

*I **wish that** you would stop bothering me.*
*The Prime Minister **argued that** neither side was right.*

The verbs in bold print in the box can also, however, be used with an alternative preposition + the **-ing** form.

*He **complained about** having to wait.*
*He **insisted on not reporting** it to the police.* (See also Unit 6.)

2 These verbs, when followed by an indirect object, are then followed by a **that** clause:

admit	agree (with someone)	mention	pretend
promise	recommend	suggest	

> He *agreed with me that* it would be difficult.
> I *promised her that* I'd arrive on time.
> He *suggested to us that* we tried a hotel.

3 Some verbs which can be followed by either an -ing form or an infinitive with to can, in more complex sentences, be followed by a **that** clause.

> She *proposed having* the meeting at a later date.
> She *proposed that* the meeting was postponed until everyone could attend.
> He *reminded us to* get there early.
> He *reminded us that* we should get to the cinema early as the film was very popular.

E Reported speech and tense changes

When we report what people have said we may have to use a different tense from the one used by the speaker.

If the reporting verb is in the past tense (e.g. *he told me that* or *he mentioned that*) then what the speaker originally said usually changes tense, as follows:

Words spoken	Words reported (She said that . . .)
'Tom needs a rest.'	Tom needed a rest.
'Things are going well.'	. . . things were going well.
'He's lost weight.'	. . . he had lost weight.
'It was a great game.'	. . . it had been a great game.
'Karen was crying again.'	. . . Karen had been crying again.
'Oliver had done everything.'	. . . Oliver had done everything.
'I'll come round later.'	. . . she would come round later.

3 First look at sentences 1–10 and find a suitable way of reporting each one from phrases a–j. Then complete these sentences, paying careful attention to sentence patterns.

a) Simon suggested . . .
b) Daniel argued . . .
c) Mr Jones threatened . . .
d) Our neighbours have invited . . .
e) The previous owners warned . . .
f) Lesley reminded . . .
g) Jim promised me . . .
h) Sheila agreed . . .
i) Mrs Winter complained . . .
j) My doctor advised . . .

1 'You really ought to give up smoking.'

....

2 'I'll definitely pick you up before eight.'

....

3 'Let's take the cat back to the vet.'

....

4 'The rain gets in if you don't shut the window tightly.'

....

5 'You're right, it's too late to phone.'

....

6 '. . . but the atmosphere won't change unless conditions are improved.'

....

7 'I'll call the police if the noise doesn't stop.'

....

8 'Don't forget that they're one hour ahead in Spain.'

....

9 'Drop in any time you like.'

....

10 'The oven didn't work from the day we moved in.'

....

F *Verbs and phrases + infinitive without* to

Some verbs and phrases in English are followed by an infinitive without **to**.

make / let
*The guard **made** us empty our cases in front of him.*
*Why won't she **let** you come with us?*

had better
*We'**d better** not leave before the others get here.*

would rather
*I'**d rather** stay here than spend an hour walking to the beach.*

NOTE: The verb **prefer** has two very different patterns:
Usually: *My sister **prefers cycling** to walking.*
But after **would**: *I'**d prefer to eat in** rather than spend all that money at a restaurant.*

COMMUNICATIVE PRACTICE

1 Message in a mime

Work with another student. Imagine you are speaking to the people in the boxes which follow.

Think of a short message that you can mime or give with a gesture to each of the people in your box. Student A: Mime your messages to your partner, who writes down what he / she thinks he has been told, advised, offered, etc. Then see if he / she understood your message correctly.

Example:

A: *You were telling me that the smoke was bothering you, weren't you?*
B: *No. I told you that there was a 'No smoking' sign in the room.*

STUDENT A   STUDENT B

1 someone who is driving
2 someone who looks fed up
3 someone who is watching television
4 someone who is angry with you

1 someone who is smoking
2 someone who has given you the wrong change
3 someone who looks lost
4 someone who is parking a car

Student B: Now mime your messages to the people in your box in the same way.

2 Complete the captions

Working with another student, look at the cartoons below and complete the caption
below each one to highlight the humour in the situation. When you have finished you will
have a chance to compare your answers to those of the original cartoonist.

1

2

3

'I still think you should ask . . .'

'Please remember . . .'   'Please stop . . .'

4

5

6

'I just have this ability to make . . .'   'You need . . .'   'I told you that I'd rather . . .'

EXAM FOCUS

1 Key-word transformation

a Complete the second sentence so that it has a similar meaning to the first sentence, using the word given. Do not change the word given. You must use between two and five words, including the word given.

1 'Why don't we go out for a change?'

Penny suggested .... for a change. **go**

2 I'd prefer to go abroad on holiday this year.

I'd .... abroad on holiday this year. **rather**

3 Were you upset that you weren't invited?

Did .... invited? **mind**

4 After trying all day, I finally succeeded in getting Mr Fisher on the phone.

I finally .... Mr Fisher on the phone after trying all day. **get**

5 I don't think you should go out with your cold.

You .... out with your cold. **better**

6 'I'll make the country a safer place,' promised the Prime Minister.

The Prime Minister .... the country a safer place. **promised**

7 'The trip is not going to be an easy one,' said our teacher.

Our teacher .... the trip wasn't going to be easy. **warned**

8 I'll need to replace my two front tyres soon.

My two front tyres .... soon. **need**

9 They kept us waiting outside for nearly two hours.

They .... outside for nearly two hours. **made**

10 I don't think we should drink the water: it looks dirty.

I .... the water: it looks dirty. **risk**

EXAM TIP 19

The verb predicts a sentence pattern

Every sentence has a verb, and you should think about the kinds of sentence patterns that can follow verbs when you do the key-word transformation task in Part 3. Many verbs can be followed by more than one pattern (infinitive, that clause, preposition, etc.). You need to think through the different options before you choose the most appropriate one.

b Complete the second sentence so that it has a similar meaning to the first sentence, using the word given. Do not change the word given. You must use between two and five words, including the word given.

1 It was good of you to come round at such short notice.

I appreciate .... round at such short notice.   **you**

2 I don't want to go if we have to stay in the same hotel as last year.

I don't want to go if .... in the same hotel as last year.   **means**

3 It would be much better if you came, too.

I .... – it would be much better.   **wish**

4 It's awful when you have to wait hours for a connecting train.

I .... to wait hours for a connecting train.   **stand**

5 I don't have the money to keep going out for dinner.

I .... going out for dinner.   **afford**

6 We weren't allowed to borrow any reference books.

They .... any reference books.   **let**

7 Jogging is much more fun than going to the gym.

I .... to the gym.   **prefer**

8 He told her that he was unhappy with the room.

He .... the room.   **complained**

9 He doesn't accept that she did it.

He insists .... it.   **do**

10 It's strange that she didn't want to come with us.

I can't imagine .... to come with us.   **her**

Unit 18 **Review unit**

> *Exam focus:* multiple-choice cloze, open cloze, key-word transformation, error correction and word formation

Part 1 Multiple-choice cloze

Important points

- This task focuses mainly on vocabulary choices rather than grammatical choices.
- It is important to try and spot what lies *behind* the question, for example: transitive / intransitive verb, countable / uncountable noun, part of phrasal verb / dependent preposition, etc.
- It is also important to try and eliminate the three wrong answers rather than going straight for the one you think is right.

For Questions 1–15, read the text below and decide which answer A, B, C or D best fits each space. There is an example at the beginning (0).

Twins

On 19 August 1939 in Piqua, Ohio, twin brothers were born (0) ....*to*........ an unmarried

mother. They (1) .... on to be adopted by different families and (2) .... up not

knowing of each other's existence. Jess and Lucille Lewis of Lima, Ohio, called their son James,

(3) .... that, 130 km away in Dayton, the other adoptive parents had also called their

new son James. It was another 39 years before James Lewis and James Springer were

(4) .... but the list of coincidences regarding those (5) .... years is astonishing.

Both had grown up with adoptive brothers called Larry and owned dogs called Toy. At school,

both excelled (6) .... mathematics but hated spelling. Both had (7) .... on

4.5 kg (10 lb) in their late teens (8) .... no obvious reason before losing the weight later.

Both (9) .... having headaches when they were eighteen which would begin in the

late afternoon and (10) .... into migraines. Both had married women called Linda,

divorced them and (11) .... remarried women named Betty. One first son had been

named James Alan, the other James Allan. Both men had been part-time deputy sheriffs,

(12) .... by McDonald's and worked as pump attendants in petrol stations. Both liked

stock car racing but hated baseball. Each year, both twins had (13) .... their families to

the same small Florida holiday (14) .... , driving there in the same (15) .... of

car and staying at hotels on the same beach.

(adapted from the *The Guinness Book of Oddities* © Guinness Publishing and Geoff Tibballs 1995)

0 A to	B got	C by	D from
1 A came	B depended	C went	D were
2 A brought	B raised	C grew	D developed

3	A unknown	B unaware	C unthinking	D unimportant
4	A rejoined	B linked	C combined	D reunited
5	A between	B interval	C missing	D disappearing
6	A of	B for	C with	D at
7	A put	B taken	C grown	D gone
8	A without	B with	C for	D being
9	A complained	B used	C started	D suffered
10	A become	B develop	C keep	D continue
11	A subsequently	B consequently	C therefore	D furthermore
12	A worked	B employed	C staffed	D occupied
13	A travelled	B brought	C taken	D spent
14	A recreation	B venue	C resort	D position
15	A label	B make	C name	D badge

Part 2 Open cloze

Important points

- This task focuses mainly on grammatical choices rather than vocabulary choices.
- You should read the whole passage through first to get a good idea of what it is about.
- Think about what part of speech is needed in the space.
- Think carefully about both the words immediately before and after the space.
- Remember that main verbs in a sentence predict the kind of patterns that will follow.
- Look for as much supporting information as you can in the text to convince yourself that you have made a correct choice.

For Questions 16–30, read the text below and think of the word which best fits each space. Use only one word in each space. There is an example at the beginning (0).

Security for the stars

Stars used to (0) ......*be*...... content with a fence around their home and an alarm system, but now some are looking for (16) .... tougher solutions. Elliot Mintz represents the estate of John Lennon, (17) .... was gunned down by a deranged fan. Now he advises other celebrities (18) .... security. 'Some stars live inside a fortress' says Mintz. 'They have all sorts of safety devices, including closed-circuit cameras and infra-red beams to see people (19) .... night. A number of them even have safe rooms, (20) .... you take at least one small area and encase it in steel so (21) .... , in the event that somebody has entered the house, a dog has been poisoned or a person who is protecting you has (22) .... eliminated, you go into the room, dial 911, and remain there (23) .... help arrives. I know one famous actress has one of these that (24) .... survive a mortar attack. It cost over $200,000.'

Bo Dietl was the (25) .... decorated New York homicide detective (26) .... history before he left the police in 1983 and set up his own security company, specialising (27) .... celebrity protection. He has strong views (28) .... his new profession and the way the stars behave. 'The client (29) .... never ask their minder to do anything else. But plenty (30) .... and they are jeopardising their own security. This is the 1990s; bad guys have guns.'

(adapted from Daniel Jeffreys, 'Minders', *Marie Claire*)

Part 3 Key-word transformation

Important points

* Remember that you should not change the word that you are given and that you must complete the second sentence with between two and five words.
* Think about the word you are given and the kind of structures you use with this word.
* In completing the second sentence think about both the changes you have to make to make the given word fit and the things that stay the same from the original sentence. For example, make sure you use tenses consistently.

For Questions 31–40, complete the second sentence so that it has similar meaning to the first sentence using the word given. Do not change the given word. You must use between two and five words including the given word. There is an example at the beginning (0).

Example: 0 I would prefer not to go out tonight.

I *would rather not go* out tonight.   **rather**

31 I've never seen a better performance.

It's .... ever seen.   **the**

32 He managed to pass his driving test at the third attempt.

He .... his driving test at the third attempt.   **succeeded**

33 I started working here four years ago.

I .... four years.   **have**

34 I think you ought to see a doctor about your arm.

You .... a doctor about your arm.   **better**

35 It's possible he didn't see the note you left.

He .... the note you left.   **seen**

36 I'm sure it isn't the engine – it's just been checked.

It .... the engine – it's just been checked.   **be**

37 I think a qualified electrician needs to look at it.

I think you need .... by a qualified electrician.   **have**

38 You only do so badly because you don't try hard.

If you .... do so badly.   **would**

39 I can't stand people talking about me behind my back.

I can't stand .... behind my back.   **talked**

40 We might go swimming so bring your swimsuit with you.

Bring your swimsuit with you .... swimming.   **case**

Part 4 Error correction

Important points

- The texts in this task are like texts written by students – so think about the type of extra word errors *you* typically make in your writing.
- You must read each line as part of the sentence it is in and think about the wider context of the text. Do not just read to the end of each line.
- The type of grammar points focused on in this exercise involve: prepositions, articles, determiners, pronouns, intensifiers, auxiliary verbs, modal verbs and linking words.
- In this exercise you are looking for extra and unnecessary words which make a sentence grammatically incorrect. You are not looking for words which *could* be removed.

For Questions 41–55, read the text below and look carefully at each line. Some of the lines are correct and some have a word which should not be there. If a line is correct, put a tick by it. If a line has a word which should not be there, write the word at the end of the line. There are two examples at the beginning (0 and 00).

Crime at Christmas

0	As Christmas was approaching I decided to give my school project the title	✓
00	'Crime at Christmas'. I had asked from my teacher if this was a good idea	*from*
41	and he agreed with that it was. I decided I would start by interviewing	
42	a policewoman. She said that the number of burglaries around Christmas did	
43	not increase as the most people think. This was because the kind of things	
44	that are being found under the Christmas tree are not those that the typical	
45	burglar is looking for. The burglar would find it difficult to sell toys. But	
46	one area although where there was an increase in crime was shoplifting.	
47	The policewoman has said that she thought this was because many	
48	people decided they couldn't afford buying the extra things they needed	
49	for Christmas. People get greedy and are more likely to take things without	
50	paying them. Another common crime she mentioned was people	
51	pretending to be Santa Claus. I laughed at this as I was thinking of	
52	people who dress up in department stores but she was not all joking. A	
53	lot of people go out onto the streets dressed as Santa so to look like people	
54	who are collecting money for charities. Of course this is not as serious	
55	as like other crimes but it is a shame people should exploit Christmas this way.	

Part 5 Word formation

Important points
- First identify what part of speech is needed in the gap and think about the spelling of this word in connection to the word you are given.
- Think about how you might have to change this word grammatically to fit the context of the text, for example, make it plural, add a negative prefix, etc.

For Questions 56–65, read the text below. Use the word given in capitals at the end of the lines to form a word that fits in the space in the same line. There is an example at the beginning (0).

World Cup mystery

The Jules Rimet Trophy, the greatest prize in (0) *professional* soccer,   PROFESSION

is more commonly (56) .... as the World Cup – a reward to one   KNOW

country and its eleven most (57) .... , idolised footballers.   GIFT

When the cup was stolen in England in 1966, (58) .... offered large   ORGANISE

rewards for its safe return. National (59) .... had to be restored to   PROUD

its rightful place. But where was the cup? The possibilities were (60) ....   END

The answer came in an (61) .... way. A man was walking his dog   EXPECT

in London when he spotted a glint, a (62) .... that lasted a second,   REFLECT

in a bundle of dirty old newspapers. He lifted the top (63) .... of   LAY

newspapers and there it was. But the still (64) .... question   ANSWER

remained: who actually stole the cup? Despite a number of (65) .... ,   SUSPECT

it was a question that the police were never to answer.

(adapted from Roger Boa and N. Blundell, *World's Greatest Unsolved Crimes*)

LEARNING
SUPPORT
UNIT